Digital Nation

Digital Nation

Toward an Inclusive Information Society

Anthony G. Wilhelm

The MIT Press
Cambridge, Massachusetts
London, England

© 2004 Massachusetts Institute of Technology

MIT Press books may be purchased at special quantity discounts for business or sales promotional use. For information, please e-mail <special_sales@mitpress.mit.edu> or write to Special Sales Department, The MIT Press, 5 Cambridge Center, Cambridge, MA 02142.

This book was set in Sabon by Graphic Composition, Inc.
Printed and bound in the United States of America.

Library of Congress Cataloging-in-Publication Data

Wilhelm, Anthony G.
  Digital nation : toward an inclusive information society / Anthony G. Wilhelm.
    p. cm.
  Includes bibliographical references and index.
  ISBN 0-262-23238-3 (hc. : alk. paper)
1. Information technology—Social aspects. 2. Cyberspace—Social aspects.
3. Information society. 4. Computers and civilization. 5. Civilization, Modern—21st century. I. Title.
HM851.W55 2004
303.48′33—dc22   2004042848

10 9 8 7 6 5 4 3 2 1

To my wonderful wife, Laura, and our children, Katie, Emily, and Andrew.

The social system is not an unchangeable order beyond human control but a pattern of human action. In justice as fairness men [and women] agree to share one another's fate. In designing institutions they undertake to avail themselves of the accidents of nature and social circumstances only when doing so is for the common benefit.

—John Rawls, *A Theory of Justice*

We cannot foresee to what extent the modes of production may be altered, or the productiveness of labour increased, by future extensions of our knowledge of the laws of nature, suggesting new processes of industry of which we have at present no conception.

—John Stuart Mill, *Principles of Political Economy*

Contents

Preface

Familiar transactions and routines based on the movement of paper and people are giving way to the flow of bits and bytes. The decision to drive to the shopping mall is tempered by the potential ease of the online purchase. Paper-based transactions—applying for college, exchanging medical records, or mailing in a voting ballot—are migrating to cyberspace. People-based transactions are also dematerializing. The government office shuts down, and the public Web site goes up; a software program replaces the guidance counselor the school can no longer afford; and remote cameras and telemonitoring equipment substitute for in-home hospice care. Spurred by the iron law of e-commerce—that moving bits instead of atoms is sure to be the cost-effective strategy—institutions, including governments, are saving time and money shifting to cyberspace.

Try getting a job without the ability to submit an online resume. How about receiving government services without owning a computer? It's increasingly difficult. Online acceptance is also becoming the norm for scholarship applications and college admission, with some places no longer permitting paper-based submissions. The digitally disenfranchised need not apply. Cyberspace's prime beneficiaries of tax-free shopping, online voting, telemedicine, and the like are already the well-heeled: they are in general big earners, likely voters, and possessors of the best medical coverage money can buy. While some type in their passwords and begin to reap digital dividends, others yet to enter cyberspace may find themselves down and out, facing economic hardship, discrimination, and disqualification without an e-mail address and knowledge of digital tools.

That computer skills and technical literacy on average enhance employability and increase earnings is a well-known fact. Lacking these talents penalizes people not only in the job hunt but also in acquiring the enormous economic benefits the Internet offers, such as lower prices and greater choice. As the mass culture migrates to cyberspace, many will be doubly disadvantaged, not just economically but socially as well. With shrinking social spending and political indifference in addressing information society issues, these divides will likely grow more acute. What's more, the emerging surveillance society, in which the latest information tools and communications networks are used to further pigeonhole ethnic and racial minorities, casts a dark cloud over the future.

No surprise, the primary driver for the headlong rush into cyberspace is economic. Public institutions are mimicking private companies, the IBMs and Ciscos, which have saved billions of dollars through paperless transactions, e-work, and virtual supply chain management. Since government coffers are empty, officials are grasping for quick and cheap fixes to meet social needs. Rather than spending a buck to print a pamphlet, maybe a Web site will do? Why complete a paper transaction when you can zap it to a customer electronically for a fraction of the cost? Who can argue with cutting corners when governments seemingly have few alternatives?

Nothing could be further from the truth. Governments and other public institutions, such as schools, are obliged to provide services without discrimination. Residents legally entitled to services cannot be denied these benefits because governments have discovered cheaper ways to offer them. How can public agencies justify shifting, say, licensing and registration online, and continue to close offices or reduce hours, when often a majority of their clients are digitally illiterate? On what basis can public schools accept applications exclusively over the Internet when many aspirants lack access to and ease with computers? Isn't it the responsibility of governments of, by, and for the people to meet people where they are, not where they would like them to be? An agency or institution providing information in PDF format only, for example, shuts out the person who can't afford a computing device with an Internet connection and who doesn't have the skills to use the tools effectively. As more and more institutions and organizations digitize their offerings, reduce staff, and close offices, we are quickly finding ourselves on the new frontier of civil rights.

Civil and political rights have been tested wherever democratic institutions foreclose people's opportunities to participate on an equal footing because of unequal access to essential computer networks and communications devices. In the Democratic primary election in Arizona in 2000, registered voters with remote Internet access were given four extra days to exercise their franchise leading up to the actual primary day when polling stations would be open. How is that for a head start? Governments are also setting harmful precedents by launching Web sites inaccessible to people with disabilities, unreadable for people with low literacy skills, and indecipherable for people who speak languages other than English. The language of technology can also exclude. In Alabama a labor agency put up billboards advertising a one-stop job assistance service, but gave only a URL as contact information. Residents were up in arms because few of the target beneficiaries could actually use the service as designed.

This book offers some ideas on how to migrate to cyberspace and avoid the pitfalls of social exclusion. I put forward a vision of a Digital Nation, a society where technology does not increasingly fray the social fabric, where everyone can take advantage of faster, cheaper, and better services. Of course, technology is not the problem. How it is used, to empower or control, liberate or enchain, is a function of human action. Social justice and fairness have been lost in the bustle to increase efficiency, often at the expense of equity. Expanding access to computing devices and communications networks is a clear first step to enhance opportunity. Increasing offerings aimed at sharpening digital literacy skills is also critical to move millions of people into the center of economic and social life.

The goal of a Digital Nation is not just to do things faster; it's to do them differently, revolutionizing the way we educate people, deliver health care, and engage in productive work. Implementing a Digital Nation vision will save the country billions of dollars over the coming years and will greatly increase quality of life as technology expands choice and opportunity. In the arenas of health delivery and e-work alone, information and communications technologies invite us to refresh our approach to rural medicine and traffic alleviation. Telemedicine applications in remote communities save lives in real-time diagnosis and treatment. Transitioning to e-work could save thousands of dollars per commuter in lost productivity and fuel consumption, not to mention have positive environmental and psychological effects. Turning a blind eye to the promise of a Digital Nation agenda, as many leaders have done, will exacerbate social inequality and lead to the demise of many communities already on the margins.

My hope is that this book will resuscitate the national debate about how we will confront the challenges and opportunities posed by a media-rich and technologically intensive society. Neglect and indecision will have far-reaching consequences in terms of lost competitive advantage, diminished productivity, and social exclusion. Relying solely on the market to arbitrate social needs, without collective intervention to foster equity and solidarity, will only exacerbate gaps in opportunity and performance. Renewed attention to building a Digital Nation requires ambitious and defensible benchmarks, goals, and time lines to hold public officials accountable for their actions and to motivate coordinated activities across a range of institutions and organizations. Restarting the dialogue is a necessary first step to recommit to a long-term agenda in which in the foreseeable future we can envision everybody contributing productively to the economic and civic vitality of a Digital Nation.

1

Digital Nation at a Crossroads

Sigmund Freud recognized three primary sources of discontent in the human condition: our struggle with nature; the deterioration of the body; and social conflict.[1] Most scientific progress and technological innovation can be explained in relation to the alleviation of one of these three problems. To ameliorate the effects of the natural world, one of the world's fastest supercomputers, operating in Yokohama, Japan, crunches teraflops of information per second in order to predict earthquakes and weather activity. Thwarting disease, extending life span, and remaking the self are key drivers of modern biotechnology research and enhancement technologies.[2] Portable, high-speed telecommunications tools are being harnessed to help monitor and regulate the body, promising to increase both access to and the quality of health services. Reducing conflict and advancing democracy have been closely aligned with improvements in communications technologies; the Internet is the latest tool to augur more harmonious relations among peoples.

The drive to stem disease and build protective shields against natural and humanmade disasters will only accelerate as new breakthroughs occur. The products of the incipient communications and biotechnology revolutions will alter our lives immeasurably in the years to come. We can only glimpse the shape of the future from our vantage point at this dawning age of instant, networked communications and the demystification of the genetic code. If the past reveals anything, it is that technological advancement will yield new conveniences and opportunities for social and political empowerment while at the same time harboring unforeseen challenges to humanity and the environment. The movement of digital bits and the harnessing of new energy sources promise cleaner transactions and processes than those of the industrial age, and the portability of intelligent devices to regulate the body and to expand communications will spread new modes of well-being and enlightenment. While it may appear that we are prevailing in the struggle against nature and ourselves and forging a healthier society, a great deal of concerted attention and action will be needed to safeguard this enterprise, particularly in democratizing access to and effective use of the critical means of communications in society.

For some, including Freud himself, the prospects for humanity's overriding its destructive penchant are grim. The decline of the nation-state, weapons proliferation, and the rise of informal terror and paramilitary networks in our time indicate that the progeny of science and invention will be uncontrollable or will control us. The mass media are full of speculations about the spread of scourges made possible by the mapping of the genetic code, or warfare against computer networks that could destabilize economies—scenarios that dim our hopes for the potential of science and technology, appropriately applied, to improve the human condition.[3] These sentiments are not unique to our age, but the tools have become so powerful as to kindle terrifying awe. The prospects for emerging technology and media to play a pivotal role in revitalizing the economy and democracy are tempered by these realities. Yet vigilant action by a broad cross-section of stakeholders could yield significant improvements in the future quality of life. Fast-forwarding to 2010 or 2020, we might be confronted by a growing surveillance society or a powder keg of global inequalities; or we might be buoyed by breakthroughs and inventions opening windows to new opportunities for civilization to flower. Which of these scenarios better approximates the society of the future will depend upon choices we make today and the degree to which citizens become engaged and voice their concerns. This book develops a case for how we might better tap the potential of information and communications technologies as drivers to expand opportunity and inclusion, a proposal to help decision makers and concerned citizens usher in a more productive and democratic society in the years to come.

We can only begin to catalog the myriad examples of the salutary uses of information and communications technologies, when organizations and individuals possess the capacity and facility to use them meaningfully and productively. Increasingly, pathways to human development intersect with technology, and examples are plentiful of individuals and organizations globally, many in dire circumstances, using a windup radio, a refurbished computer, or a mobile telephone to improve their lives in some way. In today's labor market, possessing technical skills is crucial for the job hunter to enhance the odds of finding gainful employment. Experiments with e-health show that specialists can be virtually transported to remote locations, expanding accessibility to health services while decreasing cost. And intelligent transportation and telecommuting may help untangle snarled freeways, helping commuters make up for lost productivity. A significant investment in technology-enhanced programs for health, transportation, and labor alone could save billions of dollars annually. Prudent policy-making would ensure that these efficiencies improve rather than worsen the prospects of the underclass. My checking myself out at a grocery store register or doing my banking online signals the downside of automation: redundancy. So, smarter deployment and use of these tools needs to invite not just better practice—faster, easier, more efficient—but more comprehensive and inclusive approaches to improving key areas of human life.

Investing in new technologies is no recipe for success. Simply having the tools, as is already the case in most wealthy nations, does not guarantee performance. By themselves, information and communications technologies will not bring about results; however, not possessing them in many cases will probably slow down the diffusion of innovation in the long run. Anyone who has stepped into a school knows that plowing billions of dollars into classroom educational technologies has done little on the whole to transform these efficient yet ineffective institutions. Access is necessary but not sufficient to enhance performance. Schools are often uninventive in how instruction is delivered such that technology adoption has largely hewn to established practice.[4] The tools have conformed to an outworn pedagogy in which "the filling of a pail" takes precedence over "the lighting of a fire" in the hearts and minds of learners.[5] The current mandates for high-stakes testing, for example, might mean that computers are used to drill students on multiple-choice tests, a misuse of a tool promising so much more in sparking curiosity and an appetite for learning. Educational institutions are not alone in underutilizing these tools. The productivity paradox in some businesses speaks to the misuse of information and communications technologies where organizational investments in infrastructure, if not properly orchestrated, can actually impair performance.

Training a spotlight on schools reveals that cultural norms often shape how technology is used, a reality working against the grain of the demands of the emerging society. The modus vivendi for this post-Enlightenment society is a new relationship to information and knowledge. Merely reciting facts, answering questions, following orders, and consuming media are insufficient skills to thrive in a fluid social environment. We can no longer afford to receive information and knowledge, comfortable and resigned, like the heirs of a substantial inheritance; rather, we must construct our relationship to knowledge, provisionally and tenuously, to meet human purposes. The key attributes of knowledge work and of distributed learning—teamwork, critical thinking, and adaptability—shatter the shibboleths of Enlightenment epistemology, based on the centralization of information and knowledge for individuals, institutions, and society. The acquisition of knowledge is not merely a process of collecting facts but a lifelong struggle to adapt to a mercurial and complex external world.

That technology and media are increasingly distributed and interactive puts an enormous obligation on society and individuals to navigate, adjust, adapt, and prosper in this environment. Distributed systems push information to the periphery, placing a premium on cognitive and communicative skills, such as problem solving, critical thinking, and teamwork. In manufacturing, for example, savings are realized not just in back-office, information-intensive transactions but also in reorganizing activities to make them work better. The valued employee may no longer be the one who stands on an assembly line, following orders and beating the clock, but the one who participates on a dynamic, asynchronous team contributing to a complex built-to-order production process. Interactivity also challenges individuals and organizations to be responsive and flexible, unlike the one-to-many communications approaches of the past. Peer-to-peer exchanges increase control over the communications process by sender and receiver, potentially cutting out the information broker. In El Salvador, an initiative to operate dozens of telecenters *(infocentros)* across the country allows poor businesspeople to negotiate crop prices using the Internet and peer-to-peer interactions to leverage their power over wholesalers.[6]

This book suggests a plan to harness the potential of information and communications technologies to achieve a more productive and inclusive society, a Digital Nation. Without a more robust, forward-looking national approach to weaving information and communications tools intentionally and democratically into the economic and social agenda, the nation's future is jeopardized. A Digital Nation privileges bold new experimentation to improve citizen access and effective use of new technologies while using innovative approaches to address long-standing social problems. In the health care arena, for example, a Digital Nation will optimize the use of information and communications tools to reduce the soaring costs of health services, expand access to services in remote communities, and improve the quality of diagnosis, treatment, and recovery. A Digital Nation will harness information and communications technologies to lift all boats and will not forsake populations facing serious obstacles to the realization of their life pursuits, such as immigrants, single parents, the disabled, and the incarcerated. Often these communities do not benefit from the fruits of early technology adoption because the market bypasses them. A Digital Nation will offer multiple pathways for everyone to develop the capacity and proficiency to achieve their life goals. And because human potential is often stymied by a dearth of basic literacy, a Digital Nation must customize solutions to remediation while leveraging these newfound skills to enhance communities' ability to participate meaningfully in society. These approaches acknowledge that technology is not a silver bullet; rather, it is a catalyst, driver, and powerful tool in rethinking the educational enterprise, expanding delivery of health and social services, and increasing the productivity and purpose of work. The realization of the Digital Nation, shorthand for a more productive and inclusive society, will require concerted action on the part of many stakeholders, from politicians to parents, lest the inequalities and discriminatory practices that plague the status quo be exacerbated.

Lag time in accessing and effectively using online services can be lethal, economically and socially, for groups already on society's margins. Discriminatory practices, including employment and wage bias as well as digital redlining, are pervasive in the private sphere, and even public institutions are unwittingly creating the very inequalities in opportunity that they are constitutionally beholden to thwart. Electronic government services are rolling out, for example, propelled in part by the low cost of online delivery; yet their potential beneficiaries do not always have the computers or the know-how to profit. This challenge was highlighted recently in Alabama, where a local employment office put up banners in low-income neighborhoods advertising an online job bank and offering a Web address to customers, and community leaders recoiled because the unemployed are among the least likely to have access to computers.[7] Some consumers comparison-shop online, moreover, saving money on goods and services and often avoiding sales taxes, while others must transact sales in the less competitive offline world. Using the Internet is second nature for many savvy young people, who rely heavily on the Web to conduct research and complete school admissions applications. Overseen by poorly trained teachers, other students occupy overcrowded classrooms in which computer devices are viewed as tools for geeks and nerds. Given these gaps in motivation, know-how, and technology proficiency, we must set ambitious benchmarks and accelerate the timetable for becoming a true Digital Nation.

A Digital Nation is an ambitious and achievable road map for arriving at a United States in which every resident has nondiscriminatory access to essential communications tools and information services as well as widespread opportunity to cultivate the skills to navigate a post-Enlightenment society. Achieving the vision is within our reach if leaders will focus on this issue and give it the priority it warrants. No national strategy exists to integrate the various goals for a Digital Nation beyond the silos of specific functional arenas, such as education. In the current climate a compelling vision is in abeyance that would build on the nation's proven competitive advantage and nimbleness in experimenting with new tools to enhance productivity and inclusion. Just as the vision to place a person on the moon in the early 1960s was realized as the decade closed, the dawn of a new decade motivates us to set bold goals to be realized by its close: that of universal literacy to advance creativity and unlock human potential. With the United Nations' goal to cut illiteracy in half by 2012, there is an opportunity to use information and communications technologies in an environment where the dearth of trained personnel and the magnitude of the world's illiterate population (almost 1 billion people) call for break-the-mold solutions, first to impart skills and second to translate these skills into productive engagement in the life of the larger community.

This book also articulates measurable benchmarks and timetables so that we can gauge our progress and hold institutions accountable as we journey toward a Digital Nation. The vision is by decade's end for every U.S. resident to leverage learning opportunities to become a full participant in the economic, civic, and educational life of the community. The ultimate goal of a Digital Nation, then, is outcome-driven, not focused on inputs. It is my hunch that many if not most disadvantaged Americans will find their way to the Digital Nation through some interaction with media and technology as edifying and empowering tools, if more effective and customized public policies are implemented. The drive for more skilled and credentialed workers; the threshold résumé for gainful employment; and the migration of government and educational services online means that basic skills are no longer sufficient to connect to democratic life and commercial activity. Embracing a Digital Nation ensures that no person will be left behind in the old paradigm, unable to migrate to cyberspace. It also soberly acknowledges that many people lack basic skills to participate—they cannot read, they may not speak English, they may be blind or ill—so policymakers and community leaders must be pressed to redouble their efforts to resolve these challenges with the assistance of technology where appropriate.

One of the best examples of the empowering potential of advanced telecommunications and media pertains to transformations within the disability community. Hard-fought legal victories have led to the enforcement of government mandates for organizations to provide functionally equivalent telecommunications services to the 54 million Americans with disabilities. For example, as we transition to a world of digital television, providing better picture quality and new services for consumers, Congress mandated in 1996 that captioning be made available so that everyone would have access to televised information. In the realm of telecommunications, manufacturers and service providers must make their products and services accessible to people with disabilities, if readily available. Anecdotes abound of projects and programs empowering the disabled, shifting them from marginalization to the mainstream. Funded in part by the federal government, a small project in northeast Georgia is using high bandwidth and computers with voice-enabled browsers to deliver instructional and training programs to disabled persons who need life and job skills.[8] Despite government intervention in funding and enforcement, many disabled persons are still unaffected by these miraculous tools, as are millions of others, because the political will does not exist to enforce nondiscrimination mandates and fully fund effective targeted programs.

Groups with serious challenges to their well-being—including single parents, the incarcerated, and immigrants—stand to benefit enormously from strategic investments in technology. Distance education alone is a revolutionary application for communities unwilling or unable to participate in classroom-based education. Imagine a hypothetical single mother, Maria

Gutiérrez, living in Winston-Salem, North Carolina. She has not completed high school and must juggle community college with her duties as the mother of two young children. Maria had never heard of the Internet before a recent visit to a new government-funded community technology center. She had seen many technology advertisements on Spanish-language television describing how she could save money on long-distance calls, but before a friend recommended she visit the center, she never thought about how the Internet could enable her to improve her skills, locate valuable social service information, and communicate with friends and potential employers. Maria is currently finishing her degree by taking her classes remotely in pursuit of her associate's degree. Learning technical skills and earning a degree will on average greatly enhance Maria's prospects for gainful employment.

A snapshot of the distribution of access and meaningful use of these tools shows a nation with many divisions and, most important, untapped human potential, exacerbated by the uneven deployment and application of communications. The vision of a Digital Nation is not deterministic: it does not foresee building more technology infrastructure and hoping people will come forward to use it. Rather, the vision is tied to technology's role in addressing long-standing social ills, particularly the divide in economic and civic participation, with an eye toward developing people's talents. Communications devices can also be used to tackle basic skills, such as teaching Braille or phonetics, developing building blocks with individualized learning for those who have fallen through the cracks of formal schooling.

Realizing a Digital Nation will involve a renegotiation of the social contract between government and citizens. In the early 1990s the first baby-boomer president and his technology-minded vice president set the nation on a new course, suggesting that the social contract could be better realized by testing the potential of emerging communications technologies and digital media to deliver services and streamline institutions. A policy vision of the e-commons portrayed a society in which no aspect of moribund public institutions would be untouched by technology. Indeed, the premise that these tools could influence our collective destiny in new and profound ways set the tone for the juggernaut decade of the 1990s, in which budget deficits at the beginning of the decade were soon replaced by surpluses and an enduring boom. Since the e-commons is predicated on everyone's having the ability to enter and use virtual spaces for dialogue and the delivery of services, the government immediately set to the task of building the architecture or scaffolding on which the ensuing information highway would be built. Private and public venture funds became available to seed innovation, spark entrepreneurship, and alleviate looming equity concerns. By 1994 benchmarks were in place to wire every classroom, library, health care clinic, and government agency.

While these actions were laudable, they were focused too much on inputs—in effect, a supply-driven approach to social policy—and insufficiently attuned to outcomes. Illustrated in the federal approach to education policy, the concentration on wiring classrooms took precedence over training teachers and developing content and curricula tied to standards. Rather than training a vanguard cadre of teachers and having them return to their schools to train others, many policymakers harbored a build-it-and-they-will-come mentality. This unbalanced approach is echoed in the current debate over the pace of high-speed telecommunications deployment. Industry has been pushing high-speed services to consumers, who continue to scratch their heads and wonder what qualitative difference these services make in their lives. Clearly, people need to know how to use these tools if they are to interact with them meaningfully. A concern for human-capacity building led to a focus on professional development in the late 1990s, so that teachers would be more comfortable with technology as the government was subsidizing the cost of classroom networks. Also, the notion emerged of a provisional policy solution to the challenge of achieving universal home computer and Internet access: situating government investments in communities. Programs to expand community technology centers and after-school initiatives mushroomed as the decade came to a close. This palliative first addressed the issue of generating demand among householders who otherwise would not perceive the benefits of paying for home-based technology. Second, demand-side solutions recognize that because of gaps in technical and cognitive skills among a significant swath of the underserved population, community solutions are required to exercise remediation and impart marketable skills in a supportive environment.[9] Developing content, produced in a way that was relevant to diverse communities, was critical, too, and was exemplified in some of the better community-based civic networks and public-interest media efforts. Since commercial providers are unlikely to invest in school-based markets in general, most innovative content and curriculum will be developed from the bottom up, further necessitating the diffusion of media and technology skills.

So, the nation was set on the right path, poised to develop a more integrated approach in which the transformative potential of information and communications technology would be woven into core functional areas, but it has veered off course and into rough seas. Economic and political realities thwart the realization of a Digital Nation. On the political front, because home Internet penetration is now above 50 percent, some policymakers argue it is time to retrench from government support for community-based technology programs, teacher training, and research and development. And because the Internet is ostensibly a mature industry and government coffers are emptying, some suggest it is time to step away from government-sponsored innovation. This position is at odds with the long-standing approach of policymakers concerning the appropriate role of government in supporting the rollout of information and communications technologies. Targeted subsidies for low-income telephone subscribers continue after several decades, for example, despite the fact that 96 percent of America's households are connected.[10] Additionally, the Telecommunications Act of 1996 mandates that the level of universal service should evolve and may eventually include advanced telecommunications capability, but only *after* service has been subscribed to by a substantial majority of residential customers.[11] Policymakers have recognized that intervention becomes more, not less, critical as telecommunications technology reaches a majority of households and take-up by low-income households slows. In terms of ending support for research and innovation, with technology products changing so rapidly the work of demonstrating their innovative uses for community problem solving is a moving target. Given the advent of broadband and Internet 2, along with wireless and handheld devices, next-generation funding remains essential to spur demand and spark innovation. The loss of government venture capital will result in less experimentation and entrepreneurship in harnessing technology to solve community problems and generate wealth.

Regaining momentum in achieving a Digital Nation is a critical national priority, not just a passing fancy, and will constitute a bellwether for America's success in the new century. Appeals to democratize cyberspace and invest substantial financial and human resources in its realization can be justified on economic and social justice grounds. Achieving a Digital Nation is an urgent proposition because so many people are being left out of a whole range of potentially beneficial and empowering services that if implemented effectively could improve the lives of the underclass while in the aggregate increasing productivity and saving money. Having jobs go unfilled costs industry billions of dollars annually, and raising the skills and education levels of the millions of young adults who are out of school and uncredentialed would generate billion of dollars in earnings over the course of their productive lifetimes.[12] One economic justification is that the telecommunications and media sector is one-sixth of the nation's economy and will drive future growth. While it is known that every year of formal education raises earnings by about 10 percent in the United States,[13] becoming computer- and Internet-literate also yields a wage premium, independent of educational attainment.[14] At the broader level, smart use of information technologies, particularly by business, has led to cost savings annually of $200 billion in the United States, with 30 percent of all economic growth between 1996 and 2000 attributed to enhanced productivity wrought by the information technology sector.[15] Clearly, there is a compelling national interest in fostering a universal digital literacy, boosting wages and productivity in a competitive global marketplace. The economic argument suggests that smart investment today in technology and training will reap major dividends down the road. Who would argue with the fact that the United States' leadership in the twenty-first century will continue to be predicated on its technology prowess, including the blossoming field of biotechnology? Skill in creating more intelligent machines, increasingly intermixed with biological components, may well be the industry that determines U.S. economic preeminence in future years.

At the other end of the labor market, individuals and entire communities will likely be bypassed by global economic activity if they lack technology fluency. Intellectual capital coupled with technology flows determine in large measure where knowledge work will migrate. Work shortages and unfilled positions in many industries often translate into a gap between the intellectual capital of a given community and the needs of its workforce. In places such as Los Angeles, an oversupply of underskilled, undercredentialed workers exists, creating a misfit with a dynamic economy. Indeed the achievement gap in the United States is large in comparison to those in most other industrialized nations.[16] Rectifying these inequalities and expanding the pool of the next generation of scientists, inventors, and officeholders will be a telltale for economic competitiveness in the twenty-first century. To stay competitive tomorrow's leaders will need to emerge from communities of color and include more women. When 88 percent of fourth-grade African-American students cannot read at proficiency,[17] often leading to a downward spiral of underachievement, the question of grooming tomorrow's leaders becomes tied to the resolution of systemwide failures, and the destiny of the dominant society becomes tethered to that of the marginalized.

Heirs of the social justice movement argue that human dignity and flourishing depend on everyone's having access to the necessary resources and tools to be self-governing. That telecommunications is essential to improving people's lives and achieving human dignity is captured in a statement by the UN Secretary-General and Nobel laureate Kofi Annan: "People lack many things: jobs, shelter, food, health care, and drinkable water. Today, being cut off from basic telecommunications services is a hardship almost as acute as these other deprivations, and may indeed reduce the chances of finding remedies to them."[18] Annan's statement indicates that communications, literacy, and facility with essential technologies are a set of rights that underwrite what it means to have dignity and autonomy as a human being. These social endowments are essential to exercise freedom in the world. Social advocates depend on the existing legal framework to ensure that exclusion and discrimination are overcome. The power of technology to uplift, extend, and empower has its mirror image in the plight of excluded populations who are further removed from the center of economic and civic life. So, the Constitution has been brought to bear to defend economic opportunity, voting rights, and educational advancement in the digital age. Lawsuits challenging the constitutionality of entire school districts and systems reveal a novel conception of what an adequate, up-to-date education entails, arguing for technology resources and training so that students can compete for gainful employment.

Because so much is riding on the success of the information economy, it is imperative that decision makers in government and the business community use all available levers to ensure ubiquitous access to essential tools as well as develop a variety of pathways to build entrepreneurship and training geared toward the varying needs of diverse communities. The educational and training opportunities appropriate for migrant workers and their families, for example, will be different from those of the learning-disabled or court-supervised youth, and intelligent interfaces and customized instruction can greatly benefit out-of-school and uncredentialed individuals. Since so many individuals and communities remain on the wrong side of the achievement gap, it is not surprising that social advocates have pressured government and business to step up their efforts to equalize cyberspace in the name of national security, economic prosperity, and social justice. Yet, many Americans are skeptical of spending taxpayer dollars to support what they see as other people's consumer choices. Is not the computer simply another consumer item, like a television or an automobile, whose availability resides in the domain of private choice within the marketplace? Is not the Internet simply a more sophisticated telephone, a tool that has been universally available for decades? Why all the fuss?

Early in his tenure, Federal Communications Commission Chairman Michael Powell gave a speech in which he described his opposition to the use of federal funds to subsidize Internet connectivity.[19] Saying that he, too, would like to own a Mercedes-Benz if it were not so expensive, he argued that government does not have a role in supporting consumer choices for luxury goods, items people could easily live without, such as a high-end automobile. Of course, the analogy is inappropriate; a better comparison would be government support for telecommunications and public transportation. The government may not support one's buying a sports car but it does subsidize considerably both the transportation and telecommunications infrastructures in the United States in order to expand the flow of commerce and ideas. Taxpayers expend billions of dollars annually to construct and maintain roads as well as to support intelligent transportation systems and public transportation for those who are unable or unwilling to use private transport. For all intents and purposes, these costs have become invisible to most taxpayers, who take for granted that the price of gasoline includes, on average, 42 cents per gallon in taxes, to buoy a system in which individuals and commodities can be efficiently transported.

The same is true for telecommunications. The U.S. government for years has subsidized the cost of telephone access for low-income and rural households. Part of the reason the telephone has become so ubiquitous is subsidies to make the service affordable. More recently taxpayers have begun to support the wiring of schools and libraries, so that today few publicly supported learning institutions are unconnected. The rationale is simple: the means of communications, like the means of transport, is a touchstone of a free society. Without these basic building blocks, the edifice cannot stand and the circulation of ideas is choked.

In order to boost low-income and low-achieving populations, innovative policy solutions are necessary to achieve universal literacy over the next decade. Clearly, leadership is pivotal, and the combination of powerful leadership and mobilization of a robust constituency provides the best chance of applying sufficient pressure to mine public resources in an era of fiscal belt-tightening. With the telecommunications and media sectors worth several trillion dollars, possible revenue streams can be tapped, including taxing the sale and transfer of media properties; spectrum license fees; or a communications tax on consumer purchases of media goods and services. Any or all of these would generate billions of dollars of dedicated funds to usher in the Digital Nation.[20]

In addition, the job of coordinating and implementing a Digital Nation mandate must be strengthened, both in setting benchmarks and in orchestrating a more robust national strategy that mobilizes the full force of public and private organizations. A high-ranking official to act as liaison among government departments, not just in creating interagency interoperability in the technical sense but in leveraging the substantive benefits of numerous programs across the federal government, could be useful. A national action plan would establish a putting-a-man-on-the-moon-type of goal—universal literacy over the next decade—and be a catalyst in its realization. Benchmarks would include a national plan to connect and modernize telecommunications and technology in public institutions and domiciles, including broadband access for all. It would also establish technology standards for students and teachers, and would create incentives for shifts in the way teachers are trained and where they teach. A Digital Nation plan would strengthen the school-to-work connection and expand workforce development. It would also include a strong communications component, including public service announcements in print and broadcast, to underscore the importance of a new basic literacy, mainstreaming the issue for decision makers and consumers. In 2001 a coalition of organizations, including AOL Time Warner and the American Library Association, developed an ad campaign with the slogan, "Everybody should know the basics, like how to use a computer," to motivate youths and their caregivers to get connected and sharpen their skills.[21] Future efforts should be more durable and develop the air of a movement, taking its cue from the environmental movement, where everyone begins to act in small ways to realize a larger goal, an improved quality of life for all. Transforming institutions and organizations will be pivotal in accruing maximum benefits from information and communications tools.

In any concerted effort to develop a new relationship to knowledge and technology, the needs and interests of youths and young adults in developing the Digital Nation agenda should be paramount. Millennials, those young people born since 1982, have grown up largely in a world where technology is second nature and mobile devices are extensions of their fingertips. Their frame of reference is different, and their creativity will be curtailed if the digital society is driven by a generation whose perspective is outworn. Studies suggest that students often know more than their teachers when it comes to navigating and manipulating digital tools.[22] They are often impatient with how digital literacy is taught and rely on each other to advance their skills and interests. In all informal learning environments, such as ThinkQuest and the Computer Clubhouse, children and young adults are put in the first position, and develop and design their own portfolios, with adults operating as facilitators and mentors. The Youth Employment Summit in Alexandria, Egypt, convened young people from around the world who committed themselves to a social order in which the transfer of atoms would give way to the movement of digital bits, as long as this transformation contributed to raising employment and the voice of youths, particularly those marginalized in the developing world. Since over one-half the world's population is under 25, and 80 percent live in poverty, the prospects of a new world order based on the interests of young people must address global inequalities while simultaneously encouraging entrepreneurship and innovation in the world's youth population.

Ultimately, our collective response to information inequality and the literacy gap hinges on our answer to two questions. Are there enduring divides, ones that market forces alone will not combat? And if so, is the Digital Nation such a high-salience policy concern that it warrants sustained public and private support until the vision is achieved? If there is equivocation on the first question, then clearly policymakers will take a wait-and-see approach, marginalizing the Digital Nation to a matter of diffusion curves and market forces. If there is acceptance of the first question but hedging on the second, then the issue is eclipsed by more immediate and fundamental concerns, such as fixing schools, ensuring health coverage for all, or prosecuting the war on terrorism. Leadership remains fundamental and should be framed as a matter of leveraging and integrating existing public- and private-sector investments as well as tying the discourse of digital literacy and inclusion to everyday issues of common concern. Mainstreaming this issue is key because it is not an abstract idea but a matter of economic viability, political equality, and educational opportunity. Policymakers need to advance the public-interest goals of equity and inclusion in the digital age, increasing annual investments several fold both domestically and in meeting the communications aspirations of culturally rich and economically strapped nations. And a social movement must be fostered, folded into key economic, environmental, and social struggles, where engaged citizens develop the critical mass to influence their representatives to act.

2

"Everybody Should Know the Basics, Like How to Use a Computer"

Five young commandos plunge down ropes onto the floor below, bent on infiltrating a top-secret enemy missile base. As the Latina commander barks orders at her subordinates, she focused on one eager soldier clutching a laptop computer. She peers at him to enter access codes on the computer in order to snarl the missile guidance system. His stunned look is followed by the skit's punch line, "I thought I was only supposed to carry the computer—I don't really know how to use it!"

This 30-second public service announcement was aired on Univision, a Spanish-language broadcast station, and aimed at disadvantaged young people unlikely to have home computers. Its goal was to use humor and peer pressure to motivate youths to visit a library or community center to connect to the Internet. A voice-over at the end of the spot insists, "Everybody should know the basics, like how to use a computer." A toll-free telephone number appears, connecting youths or their caregivers to a call center, where operators search for a nearby location where youths can sharpen their skills from a database of over twenty thousand libraries and community centers with free Internet access and training.

The ad represents a commitment on the part of its sponsors—technology and media companies, civil rights groups, and the library community—to elevate the national discussion over what skills are now considered basic for success while at the same time providing practical resources to at-risk youths. Although computer and online communications tools are becoming pervasive, leaders have paid scant attention to articulating a new basic literacy that both outlines the essential skills to navigate a complex society and describes the bevy of curricula and programs, formal and informal, that provide ample opportunity for people of all ages to upgrade their skills and take charge of their own learning. Employers, including information technology companies, desire an adroit workforce, an employee pool whose talents match the demands of the new economy.[1] Civil rights groups fret that the skills gap will expand, relegating millions of workers to the netherworld of underemployment and poverty.[2] And the library community is in the midst of redefining its identity as a waystation for community members thirsty not just for books but for technology.

The "know the basics" ad conveys three critical messages to its audience. First, the dearth of digital fluency has repercussions. Botching the task of jamming an enemy missile guidance system is an uncommon example of the cost of unpreparedness. But the evidence is mounting of a nation whose future prosperity is at risk, given that a significant portion of its population lacks the requisite learning and technical capacities to fulfill basic tasks. Failing to cultivate the latent talents of the millions of uncredentialed and low-skilled young people and adults costs society immensely over these cohorts' lifetimes, jeopardizing the nation's economic and political stability. The ad also reveals that a provisional remedy exists for this lack of readiness: thousands of community programs nationally provide literacy, technology, and job training of which many potential clients are unaware. Programs need to be expanded, made more relevant, and promoted more effectively, tasks imperiled by the woeful underfunding of public institutions and nonprofit organizations. Libraries, for example, are becoming more relevant by offering patrons access to the Internet and well-trained "navigators," yet budget shortfalls force library directors to make tough decisions. Many school systems remain reluctant to leverage the billions of dollars invested in educational technology in recent years by opening their technology labs and facilities after school to the wider community; they require incentives, and perhaps mandates, to broaden access. Finally and fundamentally, the ad makes the case that computers and communications devices are basic and essential, motivating stakeholders to take action to ensure that the Digital Nation be built from a solid blueprint and implemented with a broad alliance of public and private supporters with all deliberate speed.

Knowing the basics today clearly involves more than learning to read and write. There is little doubt about this, yet the status quo is often hard to bend. A movement is steadily growing that insists reading, writing, and arithmetic, the so-called 3Rs, need to be supplemented with a set of cognitive and technical skills that lead to broader participation in a complex, media-rich, and technology-reliant global society. Schools have been slow to train teachers differently or to change their curricula; adult education centers have been standoffish with technology; libraries have entered the information age demurely; and government officials have been sluggish in equipping citizens with the skills and information they need to access services that have migrated to cyberspace. Employers have cajoled schools to develop the talents of youths to solve problems, work in teams, communicate effectively, and become more facile with telecommunications tools. But most schools remain stuck in amber. A survey of over three thousand employers in Atlanta, Boston, Detroit, and Los Angeles found that a majority of newly filled jobs for non–college graduates required computer use on a daily basis, and the figure was even higher, over 75 percent of jobs, for college graduates.[3] Since most jobs require some postsecondary experience and the intense use of information technology products and services, new approaches are clearly needed to ratchet up skills substantially to meet workforce demands.[4]

The moribund state of our democratic institutions also calls urgently for a new basic literacy addressing the obligations of citizenship in an interdependent world. Telecommunications and media can be important drivers in connecting peoples and cultures in ways that build tolerance, understanding, and new forms of collective action. One youth media center in Chicago, called Street-Level Youth, works with inner-city youths in media arts and emerging technologies for use in self-expression, communications, and social change. Demonstrating a nascent manifestation of international solidarity, Street Level students traveled to Chiapas, Mexico, in 1998 and worked with indigenous youths to train them in video production to present their struggles through their own eyes to an international audience. This use of interactive media to overcome traditional borders of geography and identity signals an authentic interest among youths in media, technology, social justice, and global engagement, and should be embraced. An electronic pen-pal relationship between a high school in Seattle, Washington, and one in Port Elizabeth, South Africa, offers another glimpse at how advanced communications are cultivating mutual understanding and solidarity between diverse student groups.[5] Through videoconferencing and e-mail, students are breaking down barriers in ways that traditional media, such as textbooks and television (which often displays the U.S. identity through the distorted lens of Hollywood), often cannot. Given the monumental impact of individuals' literacy deficits, and the strong correlation between low literacy and the incidence of poverty, underemployment, voter apathy, and incarceration, it is dismaying that a clarion call has not been sounded from the highest level to mobilize the nation's resources to advance a comprehensive new basic literacy agenda. Clearly, civil society must act as the catalyst, sparking a social movement to demand a Digital Nation agenda, a regimen to accelerate economic competitiveness and broaden civic engagement in the information society.

Drinking from a Firehose

Americans gasped in 1993 when results from the first comprehensive national survey of adult literacy revealed that up to one person in two over the age of 16 lacked the skills to perform adequately many reading, writing, and computational tasks considered necessary for functioning in everyday life. Just over one-fifth of adults had very low literacy skills and usually could not successfully perform functions such as locating intersections on a street map or calculating the total cost of a purchase from an order form.[6] Another quarter of the adult population, upwards of 50 million people, were unable to perform tasks essential to support their families, perform adequately on the job, or participate in civic life. Various efforts over the years have sought to place literacy on the national radar screen, including a major millennium campaign by the National Institute for Literacy, but none has gathered momentum sufficient to affect state and national education and labor priorities. Too few resources trickle to the out-of-school population, and adult literacy and retraining remain the neglected stepchildren of the educational establishment. Given this reality, the foundation on which society currently rests is made of sand and in desperate need of shoring up.

In the early 1990s the library community identified information literacy as a critical skill to possess in an age in which the microcomputer and the five-hundred-channel universe were accelerating the need to locate, evaluate, and use information effectively. If we are to be drinking from a firehose, with billions of Web pages at our fingertips, then we should possess the skills to manage its flow. If citizens are to be active and productive shapers of their environment, then above all they need to know that they need information, possess the know-how to find and select what is appropriate, and apply what they have learned to a given situation. In a media flood in which the distinction between credible and less reliable information is obscured, and the line between education and entertainment blurs, media literacy becomes a key part of the equation to make citizens more informed and better decision makers. Too many people do not understand the political economy of the media business; and they do not know their own rights, as "owners" of the airwaves, and the obligations of broadcasters and common carriers inscribed in the law. Receiving media images minus the faculties to filter messages and decode their values can be jarring and manipulative, particularly for individuals and cultures with little experience with commercial media. The rapidly growing list of vital skills to navigate contemporary society challenges institutions and individuals to reorient, adapt, and innovate. Without relevant content, interfaces, and ubiquitous opportunities to retool, many institutions and individuals may be overwhelmed and incapacitated as they struggle to stay afloat in the new economy.

The latest approach to the literacy challenge in a world constantly redefining itself is to identify a constellation of skills and competencies, including the ability to harness information and communications tools, to meet individual, community, and organizational goals. This approach is complex and dynamic, both in defining what our relationship to these new tools and to learning ought to be and in exploiting their potential to close gaps in other cognitive and technical skills arenas. Using technology to assist with the development of other literacies—such as the use of software to teach keyboarding or Web-based systems to produce Braille—is a promising attribute of new software and portable delivery mechanisms but also raises the bar on the threshold skills needed to function in today's society. Just in terms of basic information and communications technology fluency, the Educational Testing Service (ETS) underscores five critical components of this new literacy, representing a set of skills and knowledge sequenced hierarchically to suggest increased complexity, from use for daily life skills to the tools' transformative benefits: "ICT [information and communications technology] literacy is using digital technology, communications tools, and/or networks to access, manage, integrate, evaluate, and create information in order to function in a knowledge society."[7] The ability to access information to remain informed about community problems, say, through online news, is an input that still needs to be processed to inform decision making and may well just spark the engagement of citizens in re-solving issues of personal concern.

Other approaches have cast a wider net, such as a National Research Council report suggesting that fluency with information technology encompasses three skill sets: proficiency with using today's communications tools, understanding the underpinnings of these tools, and gauging the opportunities and limitations of the devices.[8] Possessing information technology skills, for example, includes at the most rudimentary level knowledge about how to use a mouse or set up a personal computer. People having little or no frame of reference or experience with a personal computer may be disoriented, and it is not uncommon to see a first-time user pick up a mouse and point and click at the monitor, using it like a remote control. So, clearly, there is a continuum of technical fluency preceding the ability to access information as described in the ETS report. Analogous to a driver's license certifying one's knowledge of the rules of the road, the internationally recognized International Computer Driving License certification program has established a lingua franca and an international competency standard for computer literacy now recognized in about ninety countries. In terms of appreciating the limitations of the media, in focus groups with underserved families some perceive a networked computer as an intelligent device in which resides a sort of deus ex machina, so that inquiries will yield unequivocal answers rather than information to be processed and integrated into one's own frame of reference.[9] Clearly, understanding what it means to program a computer or to utilize a search engine is important to comprehend how systems work the way they do.

The most compelling and high-level case for immediate implementation of a new basic literacy came in a speech from German Chancellor Gerhard Schröder at a summit on twenty-first-century literacy, held in Berlin, Germany, early in 2002. Sponsored by the then AOL Time Warner Foundation and the Bertelsmann Foundation, two of the world's largest media conglomerates, the summit sponsors' goal was to elevate the issue to the level of international prominence and concern. A white paper crafted for the event outlined four touchstones for twenty-first-century literacy, including technology and information literacy, media creativity, and social competence, the latter outlining the important consequences users must consider in using the medium, such as the responsible use of the Internet.[10] Highlighting the creative potential of networks and mobile devices is key as young people fashion a vanguard movement, upending and transforming what mainstream media have forged.[11] For Schröder the new century represents an epochal shift in the unfolding of human history, with a focus on human development, literacy, and education as its critical touchstone. The groundwork for this focus on learning is a commitment to a new culture of lifelong learning and the development of a broader conception of literacy able to support a more vibrant democracy in the years to come. What is awakening in the minds of leaders is the notion that these tools must be embraced as an issue of first priority although their full flowering will vary depending on geography, culture, and context.

Returning to the hypothetical example of Maria Gutiérrez, imagine she has just landed a job and thus must find child care for her two kids. Assuming Maria is new to a community and does not have family members or neighbors to rely on for advice or as caregivers, she needs to recognize the need to search for potential child care providers, be able to identify options, discriminate among them, and act on this information. As governments and private businesses move information services online, it will be increasingly difficult for Maria to pick up a phone or seek paper-based information to receive suitable answers to her questions. She will be forced to migrate to cyberspace. The close-down effect, the steady transfer of information and services from paper formats and physical locations to cyberspace, ratchets up the importance of the widespread diffusion of information and communications technologies in everyday life and the technical and learning competencies to use them.

Because Maria happens to live in the state of North Carolina, she might benefit from a database-driven e-government Web site called NC@ YourService, which provides a wealth of child care information by type and quality of facility as well as by geography. So she might type in her zip code, choose the type of center for which she is looking, and select the level of standards the center meets. She could also quickly determine whether she is eligible for child care assistance and whether her center of choice accepts vouchers. Of course, the use of this powerful tool depends on Maria's broader literacy skills, including her experience with the Internet, in other words, her ability to use a search engine to access the state's Web site, evaluate it to determine whether it is useful to meet her needs, manage the information she collects through the database, integrate it into her frame of reference, and develop a ranking of her top selections. These twenty-first-century literacy skills are imperative to master as economic activity and public services migrate online.

The success of her enterprise also hinges on underlying technical and cognitive skills, including her ability to compare centers and to locate and transport to the center and register her child. A Digital Nation will require more, not less, of individuals and organizations. At least until the age of intelligent machines arrives, connectivity will place greater responsibility on the individual to make unaided decisions. Whether it is buying a house without a realtor through an online mortgage broker or trading stocks without an intermediary, or even taking an online course, accountability falls squarely on individuals to navigate transactions and assume responsibility for their own learning, often without the hand-holding or the special knowledge of trained professionals.

Undoubtedly Maria's success will depend on her ability to marshal her own resources to navigate this online world, but her community and government also can play pivotal roles in providing digital opportunities. Governments have just begun to roll out online services to their clients. North Carolina is a leader in this; unfortunately, most others have a paucity of manageable information and easy-to-use services.[12] The architects of these services often have people like themselves in mind when devising the interfaces and content rather than users whose language, literacy level, disabilities, or cultural needs may differ from their own. Digital divides remain as obstacles to universal adoption of e-government as large populations continue to lack the basic tools and capabilities to be full participants in the online world. So, if Maria does not have a computer and speaks only Spanish, she will likely be unable to avail herself of certain services to which she is legally entitled.

Sharpening new skills, such as computer and Internet fluency, problem solving, and media literacy, does not supplant the need to develop more traditional skills. Even as learning becomes more self-directed online, learners still need to read, write, and do math adeptly. The relationship among these literacies resembles a rope of strands, the intertwining of discrete skills that, when combined, strengthen the whole. Clearly, one cannot navigate the Internet in its current incarnation as a text-based medium without the underlying cognitive skills. Conversely, information and communications tools can individualize instruction to raise literacy and enhance remediation strategies. For people with learning or physical disabilities, or for those who may have fallen through the cracks of formal learning, these tools offer particular promise in creating a virtuous cycle to reinforce skill development through customization.

The technology approach of the Puente Learning Center in East Los Angeles, California, typifies this virtuous cycle. Working with many non–English speakers, and affirming the importance of exposing the entire community to computers and information networks, the center's staff uses an innovative authoring program to teach English as a Second Language (ESL).[13] Developed by the Duke University Computer-Assisted Language Learning Project, the easy-to-use computer-based system enables teachers to customize instruction with their own subject material, presentation style, and questions. In turn, students can practice grammar, sentence structure, vocabulary, and reading at their own pace until the lessons are mastered. Students with no computer experience first learn to keyboard using a computer-based typing course and work up to sophisticated multimedia language acquisition systems with the assistance of trained facilitators.

Decision makers and the public are more likely to view information and communications tools as basic and essential, like electricity, the more they experience benefits resulting not just from the dictates of the economy but also from the power of the technology itself. A real-life example of a Web site offering tremendous opportunity to people in need is the Benefits Checkup, a service that invites individuals to fill out a brief questionnaire (no identifying information such as social security number or name is required) and to receive a "results overview," with a list of potential benefits for which they are already eligible.[14] Every weekend for five years, Wanda Baker drove 255 miles from Silver Spring, Maryland, to North Carolina to care for her elderly parents, both of whom had suffered strokes. After years of shouldering the costs of home health assistance, Wanda discovered the Benefits Checkup at her workplace and found that her parents were eligible for free home health assistance under Medicare. According to the National Council on the Aging, as many as 5 million older Americans are not availing themselves of entitlements, tax breaks, transportation, and the like because they simply are not aware of these benefits. Happily, Wanda had access to a computer and Internet connection and, serendipitously, she actually worked at the National Council on the Aging, the online tool's primary developers. Using information technologies is clearly empowering, increasingly so for the nation and the world.

Changing our relationship to information and knowledge is a tumultuous enterprise, particularly given the resistance of incumbent forces. The best example of this phenomenon is in education, where computers are sometimes used as expensive typewriters, elaborate encyclopedias, or overwrought calculators and at other times as empowering platforms for group learning. Often computers are used to drill and repeat, and access to the Internet is used as a reward when students finish their assignment early. In the climate of high-stakes testing, computers are wielded as more efficient and accurate instruments to replace the graphite pencil. Such use fails to put the learner at the center of a dynamic process of constructing a meaningful relationship to knowledge.[15] One example of leading-edge youth-centered e-learning is ThinkQuest, a global network of students and teachers where young people learn, teach, mentor, discover, research, and grow, working in teams harnessing the power of the Internet, as the organization's home page suggests, to "learn the 21st century skills of online collaboration, Internet research, asynchronous project management and Web communications."[16] One award-winning sixth-grade team from Visalia, California, created a breathtaking Web site on the threatened ecosystem of the California sea otter using, among other tools, digital cameras, Adobe Photoshop, and professional Web-authoring software. These elementary school kids are likely to master most of the tools needed to compete in tomorrow's economy, including the ability to adapt to a world in which a large percentage of future jobs have yet to be invented. They are also addressing real-world problems in their communities, able to connect their experiences in the classroom with the needs and challenges of their local environment.

Desert Island Wish List

Skills are specific to an epoch. Just as a Neanderthal probably needed self-made stone tools when hunting game, the contemporary jobseeker in possession of marketable skills can find success in the external environment. While a Neanderthal surely acquired skills modern peoples will never possess (how many of us can skillfully flake stones to make sharp tools?), modern peoples in search of gainful employment might find that having the right certification does just fine. As late as the twentieth century, survival skills still revolved around physical strength, whereas today intellectual and technical prowess are linchpins of information and knowledge economies.

Over long stretches of human history, requisite skills have remained relatively constant, punctuated by breakthroughs in the appropriation of natural resources, such as what defined the transition from the Paleolithic to the Mesolithic age. Over thousands of years chipping stones to sharpen tools gave way to the making of microliths, implements with multiple sharp edges used as blades, axes, or arrows. Setting upon nature and improving human implements continue to define eras, from the industrial age, driven by steam and coal, to today's hyperaccelerating digital economy. Information and communications technologies have come to shape our age and infuse capitalism's veins and capillaries, and hence steer our learning institutions and workplaces toward sharpening digital skills. Yet the technical requirements of the information economy are such that the skills learned in school or on the job quickly become obsolete, no longer sufficient to ply a trade. Lifelong learning and retraining become critical levers to enhance productivity. But also, schools must understand and inculcate the underlying sets of durable skills required to find success across a range of professions and sectors in the modern economy, such as multistep problem solving, the management of complexity, personal responsibility, and teamwork, perhaps weaving these skills into teaching core academic competencies.

Technology is increasingly a vital ingredient for success across sectors and economies. Age-old traditions, such as dairy farming, are brushing up against the modern world, and savvy farmers across the globe are using technology to monitor milk content and the market to survive and prosper. In rural India, for example, a company has introduced an automatic milk collection system used in hundreds of dairy cooperatives, collecting, processing, and marketing milk through a computer-aided process that takes a fraction of the time of a manual one.[17] Members of the cooperative present a plastic identification card, a milk sample is quickly analyzed, and a receipt is printed in order for the farmer to collect payment. Countries cloistered away and closed to the outside world, such as Bhutan, have opened their society to the Internet.[18] And nations with few resources— even those battling the widespread ravages of AIDS and civil war, such as Botswana or Sierra Leone—recognize the need to advance their citizens with the assistance of these tools.

Despite the success stories, people still argue that technology is a luxury, a tool inessential for survival. Surely, anyone stranded on a desert island would pass over the prospect of salvaging a computer from a shipwreck in favor of securing a bowie knife to make shelter and to kill game for food. Balking at "overreliance" on information and communications technology, critics argue that in the hierarchy of needs, having shelter and food precede whatever benefits could possibly accrue from networking indigent communities. Perhaps the argument is made most forcefully in the realm of international development, where many practitioners and experts decry the application of technology to solve the range of development challenges. Why donate computers when people are starving? might be an extreme expression of this viewpoint.

Even Bill Gates, the titan of the computer software industry, has fueled the zero-sum thinking between basic needs and technology. In a conversation with Scott Shuster from *Business Week* magazine at an October 2000 conference in Seattle, Washington, Gates expressed his personal commitment to eradicating infectious diseases and suggested that basic health and literacy were prerequisites for economic development and technological advancement. He resisted the approach of others at the conference who suggested sustained economic development is correlated with improved health and quality of life, including literacy development. For Gates, "health first, then literacy; once you have literacy then you have a chance to bring in the new tools of communication."[19] In the course of the interview, he said his foundation allocates approximately 30 percent of its resources to information technology–related grantmaking and 60 percent to global health, suggesting that health spending should trump technology investment but that the latter should be supported on a sliding scale depending on the general level of health, literacy, and well-being of a given community and society.

A somewhat frivolous response to the desert island scenario is, Would not the castaway benefit mightily from a communications device in order to accelerate a rescue? More seriously, anybody in a society with a 911-type emergency communications service knows that the telephone can relay lifesaving information to respondents. Historically, telephone companies as common carriers were sued for untoward circumstances resulting from disconnection, such as a child's dying when the phone failed to work and a physician could not be reached, or a retailer's losing business when clients could not ring up the store.[20]

More philosophically, the yearning for communications and companionship seems as basic as any in the hierarchy of human needs. If Aristotle is right, and humans are by nature social creatures, then would we not be less than human if we led lives of isolation? The 1980 UNESCO report *Many Voices, One World* is a standard-bearer for articulating the value of communications for addressing democracy and human development in our times. With its famous members, including Sean MacBride, the Irish Nobel Peace Prize laureate, and Gabriel García Márquez, the 1982 Nobel laureate in literature, the International Commission for the Study of Communication Problems projected an aura seldom seen in the development and release of United Nations reports. Articulating a forward-looking vision for communications, the report concludes with the firm conviction that "communication is a basic individual right, as well as a collective one required by all communities and nations. Freedom of information—and more specifically, the right to seek, receive, and impart information—is a fundamental human right; indeed, a prerequisite for many others."[21] The report is an eloquent voice for the inextricable link between the freedom of communications and the liberty of the citizen, a link corroding in our times because of the growing commercialization and concentration of media.

The effective truth of living in an interdependent world is that subsistence living in isolation from the community of nations and global civil society is quickly disappearing. John Donne wrote, "No man is an island,"[22] and this is true today, when global environmental, health, and development challenges require real-time collective responses. As modern chaos theory tells us, activity in one part of the globe might easily affect the climate on the other side of the world, necessitating stronger transnational public communications and arenas for collective action. Just as the transcontinental railroad in the nineteenth century created boom towns through which the railroad passed and ghost towns in communities far from its thunderous roar, not being touched by advanced communications tools is disastrous, particularly for rural and underserved communities.

Even cultures and groups wishing to preserve their independence from a dominant society are dependent on external forces. Threatened societies are turning to information and communications technologies to protect and preserve their heritage. The National Indian Telecommunications Institute (NITI), for example, is using technology to save the Comanche language.[23] To preserve and disseminate the language to the young, NITI is producing an interactive dictionary of the Comanche language, including audio clips of Comanche elders pronouncing sounds and words, an essential safeguard for a language fast disappearing from Comanche homes and schools.

At every level of decision making, leaders acknowledge that these tools are basic and essential to survive and prosper in the twenty-first century. When UN Secretary-General Kofi Annan compared the importance of telecommunications to having drinkable water or health care, he was making two fundamental political points. First, these rights are guaranteed protection, so people's free speech rights should be respected and defended wherever they are trampled. Second, the ability of individuals and communities to exercise their right to communicate should be supported by the family of nations, including providing resources to develop communications infrastructure globally, even in the hardest-to-serve communities. As the United States and other nations dedicate themselves to universal service—that is, ensuring that every household has the essential communications technologies of the day—they should demonstrate their commitment to this fundamental value through robust support for nations without the resources to realize this basic right. Universal service would then be truly universal.

In a 1995 speech at the opening ceremony of the Seventh World Telecommunications Forum and Exhibition, former South African president, Nelson Mandela, stated, "In the twenty-first century, the capacity to communicate will almost certainly be a key human right."[24] This sentiment was echoed among senior U.S. policymakers, such as former Assistant Secretary of Commerce Larry Irving, who attested in July 1999 that the digital divide is "now one of America's leading economic and civil rights issues."[25] Even industry leaders agree: former AOL Time Warner CEO Steve Case stated in a May 1999 speech at the Leadership Conference on Civil Rights policy conference that there was merit in viewing access to the Internet as a key civil rights issue in the coming years.

Above all, these proclamations are predicated on the belief that emerging information and communications technologies are essential for individuals and communities to fulfill their life pursuits. This belief is key in defining a political conception of the capabilities that persons must possess in order to have a viable opportunity to participate in economic and civic life. Across the community of nations, computer facility and Internet accessibility are indicators of a conception of development that is steadily gaining currency, included as they are in the UN Millennium Development Goals.[26] To suggest that an Internet connection or a personal computing device is as necessary as a telephone arouses society's interest in establishing the conditions in which such technology becomes available universally, including to low-income and rural communities. Whether the democratic and comprehensive plan of embedding a Digital Nation agenda in the larger context of human development wins the day depends on whether policymakers see through to a new approach in addressing chronic problems of poverty, social exclusion, and underdevelopment.

One arena where new thinking is germinating is in heated debates over remedies for unequal access to educational opportunities across communities. In recent years, parents, concerned citizens, and advocates have appealed to courts in several states to demand fiscal parity and educational "adequacy," such as better school facilities, expansion of early childhood programs, and salary increases to attract and retain high-quality teachers.[27] Funded largely by local property taxes, the educational system is markedly unequal and places low-income and rural students without a viable opportunity to participate fully in the life of the larger community. Now that Internet use in schools is becoming a magnet for students, the conversation about what facilities are adequate to achieve educational equity and true opportunity is beginning to envelop educational technology and virtual learning experiences.

While international law and the law of nations—whether it be the UN Charter, the venerable first amendment to the U.S. Constitution, or the updated language of the 1996 Constitution of the Republic of South Africa, guaranteeing the "freedom to receive or impart information or ideas"— ascribe a privileged place to the right to communicate, the realization of these political ambitions is often stymied by economic and social forces. In the United States, for example, constitutions and key legislation safeguarding the right to an adequate education and universal telecommunications service have not mitigated one of the world's largest technology and educational achievement gaps between haves and have-nots. As nation-states move from declaratory statements to "e-strategies," they are faced with many choices and challenges to developing regulatory certainty, competition, adequate legal structures, universal service provisions, and new avenues to expand learning and human-capacity-building opportunities for their people.

Some nations are leapfrogging their neighbors with leadership focused on creating the right climate for information and communications technology to take root and grow. In Costa Rica, for example, the entire nation is now networked to the last mile with fiber-optic technology, an infrastructure development plan that is consonant with and fully integrated into the nation's human development, economic, and environmental goals.[28] With its aggressive goal of providing all children access to e-mail and attracting high-technology investment in biotechnology as well as information services and computing, this tiny nation has catapulted itself into the forefront of the information society. Other examples of technology development in Estonia, Finland, and Singapore suggest the potential of these information and communications tools to raise standards of living of all.[29]

Walking to Timbuktu

Elevating the issue to the level of a basic necessity signals that political and industrial leadership and resources need to be leveraged to ensure that populations gain access to critical services as well as a broader array of formal and informal educational opportunities to usher in a Digital Nation. It is critical that benchmarks be established to measure progress and hold decision makers accountable for their action (or inaction) over time. It may be useful to examine benchmarks and timetables along several dimensions of the problem, what we might call its width, height, and depth. Width refers to the quantity of devices per user across various institutions, including the home. So, the Clinton administration's goal to wire 100 percent of classrooms is in a sense one-dimensional, a supply-side focus on infrastructure. At the global level, increasing access to telephones and personal computers per thousand residents are fixtures of the UN Millennium Development Goals, alongside eradicating hunger and reducing child mortality, signaling the pivotal role of information and communications tools as key development tools while admittedly addressing only one facet of the role of communications in improving people's lives. Sometimes goals are rather vague, such as one publicized several years ago that every person in the world ought to be no more than half a day's walk from a telecenter, which must have seemed to many folks in sparsely populated parts of the globe as tantamount to walking to Timbuktu. Another dimension of a Digital Nation agenda, height, is benchmarking strides in literacy development, broadly understood as the set of technical and cognitive capabilities needed to function in an information society. The UN Literacy Decade aims to close the education gap, stimulating public and private activity to increase literacy levels 50 percent by 2015, with new technologies being key drivers in the international plan of action developed to reach this ambitious target.[30] A new provision of national education policy in the United States states that every eighth-grader must be technology-literate regardless of socioeconomic status or race.[31] The Partnership for 21st Century Skills has been charged by the U.S. Department of Education with fleshing out this provision. Its definition is broad, including the new literacy skills young people will need in order to partake of economic, civic, and social life. As states apply this new provision in the creation of standards and the implementation of diagnostics to test performance, clearly the way children are educated will begin to change, both in integrating these new skills into traditional subject areas and, more fundamentally, in transcending disciplines and school walls in pursuit of a more rewarding relationship to knowledge.

This notion of transforming institutions leads to the third dimension of a Digital Nation agenda, depth. Depth indicates that institutions need to go beyond procuring technology and training staff; they must also rethink their architecture, reinventing themselves as communications makes this reinvention possible and desirable. A project in the United Kingdom called Not-School.net illustrates how technology can revolutionize learning, supporting a virtual learning community of young people who for a number of reasons, such as pregnancy, bullying, or disaffection, were excluded from formal education.[32] The project exists almost exclusively online, where young people engage in self-directed work with cybertutors to develop their self-esteem and ignite their interest in learning through topics of interest to them. The program leads to formal accreditation and has the side benefit of introducing digital literacy skills to siblings, parents, and caregivers. Because of its success, the model is branching out to educational authorities across the United Kingdom and overseas and, not unlike other successful informal enterprises, is receiving attention from the formal establishment in its desire to acknowledge and partially underwrite these efforts.

It has been no small feat connecting so many classrooms, libraries, households, businesses, and community centers to the Internet over the past decade, albeit diffusion remains uneven by geography and economic strata. Virtually all of the nation's classrooms and libraries are connected;[33]

over half of all households can access online services;[34] workplaces offer millions of employees e-mail accounts; and nonprofit community centers are plentiful, with neighborhood residents availing themselves of computer applications and Web training. A decade of investment and the hottest economy on record between 1992 and 2000, however, did not bring everyone online. According to reports, a digital divide continues unabated.[35] If current trends continue, a problem will exist at decade's end with substantial pockets of the U.S. population unplugged from a Digital Nation. Thus, the creation of benchmarks must also be accompanied by reasonable time lines lest the Digital Nation never be realized.

In remote areas of the country and among the very poor, for example, reliable telephone service is unavailable, and tens of millions of people are complete strangers to the world of e-commerce, instant communications, and online social engagement.[36] A new hi-tech divide also looms as high-speed broadband services are deployed, providing faster connections to the Internet, allowing consumers to watch and upload video, take courses online, and even send their vital signs to a health clinic for diagnosis. Because these services are expensive, their uneven rollout threatens to exclude millions of individuals from such killer apps as e-health and distance education until long after these have become the staple of health and education service delivery. With the market capitalization of information technology and telecommunications in the doldrums and Wall Street investors increasingly diffident, the optimists of the late 1990s who forecasted the closing of the digital divide are yielding to more realistic appraisals of when, if ever, the technology gap will close. Meanwhile, other regions are still awaiting their first telephone call or high-speed Internet connection. At a regional conference in Bamako, Mali, to prepare for the Geneva phase of the World Summit on the Information Society, African leaders articulated goals for the continent's broad participation in the global information society. Yet these goals need to be tied to real foreign aid and investments as well as coordinated action in building the capacity of indigenous groups to construct legal, regulatory, and technical frameworks, including privacy and security protections, in order to make progress.

Timetables for reaching universal diffusion of essential information and communications services are critical; otherwise, the default position of most will be to rely on market forces (where incumbent providers dominate) to arbitrate technology adoption. Some decision makers will balk at a Digital Nation agenda, for example, claiming that the problem is more illusory than real. The argument from critics regarding Internet diffusion usually goes, If the adoption curve is halfway along, then the question really is not whether households will come online but how long it will take until the market serves everybody. Those who believe that these are merely consumer goods suggest that the issue is more about have-nows versus have-laters than about an enduring information underclass. With price points coming down for computers, for example, the public can springboard to the Internet. So what is the problem, say the detractors? Those who claim that the issue is about have-nows versus have-laters make a leap of faith: that the market will serve everybody in short order. They ignore penetration lags shutting out whole communities and groups from the benefits of advanced communications, possibly through the better part of this decade and beyond. The crux of the issue, then, is not how long it will take before the gaps close but rather what the likely impact is of excluding millions of Americans from the major artery of information, communications, and commerce. Do not the detrimental effects of e-exclusion merit some sort of public response?

While computers and Internet service are becoming as ubiquitous as television sets in high-income households, this is a far cry from acknowledging that diffusion patterns now resemble a random cross-section of the U.S. population. As with other technologies, there is a saturation of upper- and middle-class adopters, and a protracted time period ensues in which adoption rates for poor households increase incrementally. With the telephone, for example, it took eighty-three years after its invention in order for diffusion to approach universal levels, and significant gaps remain along income, ethnic, and geographic lines. Even the most optimistic market research suggests that low-income Americans continue to be hard to reach and are coming onto the network at rates much lower than middle-class Americans. Today, some households with modest incomes are forced to choose among their mobile phone connection, cable service, land-line telephony, and Internet service. Some of these services may be bundled, but throwing in the high cost of broadband service forces consumers to make choices little understood by researchers. One study shows Internet growth beginning to plateau, a historic occurrence for a medium whose diffusion had skyrocketed for several years before the 2000 economic downturn paralyzed the U.S. economy.[37] The gaps between bottom and top economic quartiles in Internet access are yawning, and they grow over time. Only one in four of America's poorest households was online in late 2001 compared to eight in ten homes earning over $75,000 per year.[38] With the next-generation broadband divide, moreover, almost twice as many urban households were connected to the Internet via high-speed broadband access in mid-2001 compared to rural communities; and the divide grew precipitously over the previous year.[39] And broadband prices are now two to three times what they are for telephone or Internet service.

Gaps in Internet access along educational lines continue to grow and highlight the difficult challenge of using the Internet to bring learning skills to the least educated. Significant gaps exist not only between college graduates and those without a high school degree but also between college graduates and high school graduates. Between 1998 and 2001 the divide between those at the highest and lowest education levels increased 11 percent.[40] The strong correlation between educational attainment and Internet access is revealed in the fact that 84 percent of persons with more than a bachelor's degree were connected to the Internet in 2001, compared with only 13 percent of those without a high school degree.[41] The further one steps down the rungs of educational attainment, the fewer the number of Internet users, with persons with minimal formal educational training basically without access to the tools required for learning in the twenty-first century, let alone literacy skills sufficient to use these tools effectively.

Beginning in 2001 the confluence of several significant factors began to bring a digital inclusion agenda to a grinding halt: reductions in public and private funding; depleted telecommunications sector capitalization following the dot-com crash; the slowing of U.S. sales of computers and Internet services; and the absence of a killer app to spur demand for high-speed services. Clearly, this economic cycle indicates that rather than receding from the policy agenda, a Digital Nation mandate ought to be a mainstay of national policymaking for the foreseeable future. Otherwise, the inclusive and high-performing vision of a Digital Nation will be realized solely as a function of the vicissitudes of market forces.

3

A Faustian Bargain for the Digital Age

Near the peak of its market worth in late 1999, Cisco Systems conducted an internal review of an experiment begun in 1994 to realize cost savings from Internet-based internal business processes, such as consumer care and supply chain management. Eager to export its credo—that information technology investments benefit companies that array their business practices virtually—Cisco self-reported cumulative cost reductions amounting to 5.3 percent of its end-period revenues.[1] For any company looking for an edge, cost savings of 5 percent are significant (approximately $650 million, in this instance) and translate into greater shareholder return. If Cisco is a harbinger of e-business, then other companies will need to achieve some approximation of Cisco's success in order to compete. According to one estimate, manufacturers could expect about $100 billion in savings over a similar four-and-a-half-year period.[2]

Cisco's example is being followed by organizations, private and public, large and small, striving to realize significant cost savings and productivity gains with smart investment in information technology. Public-sector schools and governments as well as businesses of all persuasions invested heavily in technology during the boom economy, and stalwarts in leaner times hope to parlay that investment, providing quality service with reduced operating budgets. In the mid-1990s, for example, the notion of reinventing government over time led into e-government as a way to streamline agencies and shave costs. A bestseller in 1993, *Reinventing Government*, by David Osborne and Ted Gaebler, referenced information technology only three times in the entire book. Eight years later, the Harvard professor Jane Fountain published *Building the Virtual State*, a manifesto steeped in technological prescriptions for repairing flaws in government organization. Major legislation enacted by the 107th Congress, moreover, established a broad framework for strategically harnessing the $45 billion the federal government spends on information technology, including requiring federal offices to use Internet-based information technology to enhance citizen access to government information and services. With federal and state budgets in shambles, officials are eager to conduct electronic service delivery and paperless transactions at a fraction of the cost of traditional paper service.[3] In the ballooning health care sector, similar expectations are building, and massive savings are possible in the coming years as providers, including governments, strive to reduce back-office costs and extend services into remote communities without fixed-cost bricks and mortar. Even school systems are not immune to technology's prescription, both in streamlining procurement and in envisioning schools without walls. If designed smartly, the virtual school, clinic, or government may well be an appropriate extension of and complement to high-quality service delivery; but vigilance is required to ensure that people's essential learning, health, and social service needs are not sacrificed at the altar of efficiency.

Amazon.com's chief executive officer, Jeff Bezos, exemplifies the efficiency-maximization argument when he says that moving bits instead of atoms is sure to be the cost-effective solution to any problem. For Bezos, his company's meteoric rise is a vanguard for the retail sector, harnessing e-commerce as a strategy for profitability; the key resides in moving bits, not atoms—that is, keeping people and paper stationary to the extent feasible and instead relying on the flow of bits and bytes. Not only is the business model solid, according to Bezos, but the positive side effects of e-commerce are undeniable. Centralizing distribution reduces overhead; virtual marketing eliminates needless display; and these two forces—antithetical to the environmental casualties of a shopping mall culture—reduce automotive emissions and landfill (all else being equal). With the virtual retailer beginning to demonstrate success, is the virtual school, the virtual hospital, or virtual government just around the corner?

Taking a shrewd look at efforts to realize massive productivity gains and cost savings due to smart investment in technology is essential to gauge the trade-offs for a Digital Nation agenda. Some of the cost-saving estimates, both in business-to-business and business-to-consumer transactions, are impressive and should not be shrugged off lightly. But some champions of e-commerce like Bezos fail to note some of the negative consequences of information age activities, which are certainly less apparent than the havoc caused by the ascendance of industrial age production but are nonetheless real. The effects of long-term exposure to toxic emissions and electromagnetic radiation generated from electronics production are poorly understood.[4] When computers and peripherals die, moreover, they are shipped to developing nations to be buried, emitting noxious poisons into the land as their remains are scavenged.[5] And who knows what the displacement of atoms by bits ultimately portends: since human beings are made of atoms, will intelligent machines replace them in the name of efficiency,[6] just as greedy landowners and the mechanical cotton picker expelled sharecroppers from the South in the mid-twentieth century?[7]

Taking Bezos's basic premise regarding the virtues of centralized distribution and e-commerce, one can easily imagine a counterpoint in which a town or community loses its local bookseller, put out of business by another retailer's economy of scale and low overhead. Imagine that around this bookstore, the townspeople had congregated, adding to sociability and trust. Is there not something frayed in the fabric of community when a virtual business becomes the largest bookseller in town and the only social capital levied from a book purchase is a 30-second encounter with a UPS driver as your item is delivered in a plain brown box?

The comparison between businesses and the public sector is clearly imperfect because businesses can pick and choose their customers and shed employees as economic cycles contract and new labor-saving devices are invented. Governments and learning institutions are legally obligated to serve everyone without discrimination. A school is not a business. Nor is the polity. Schools and governments cannot be fickle. Industry innovations trickling down to public institutions must be filtered through the sieve of efficiency and equity. This necessary calculation—the requirement for fair and equal regulation of society—is clearly a catch-22 for the public sector. Governments cannot realize cost savings from paperless transactions unless everyone is online; schools cannot harness these tools to extend learning into remote communities with rampant digital divides; and hospitals and health centers cannot broaden the availability of e-health applications if rural or elderly patients lack telecommunications services or are apprehensive about using them. All too clearly, a Digital Nation's imperative is to increase equal opportunity as well as convenience. The push for equity, of course, can hamper efficiency. Politicians face the dilemma that they must show short-term efficiency gains as a yardstick for electoral success. This myopic approach, however, fails to account for the fact that equity issues, such as historic discrimination against racial and ethnic minorities, can arrest performance gains, demanding a longer-term strategy for economic and community development. Is this not a fair price to pay to sail closer to democracy's shores?

A Faustian Bargain

This book harbors no illusions: achieving a Digital Nation is a Faustian bargain. With any bargain, one receives something in exchange for giving away something of value. In Goethe's tale of Faust, the protagonist makes a deal with the devil, gaining the powerful gift to act decisively and to master nature unceasingly. Near the end of Goethe's tragedy, Faust has erected a citadel to human achievement: he drains swamps, builds a modern city, and erects dikes to protect it against nature's ravages. What he irretrievably loses is a reverence for what fades away because of his striving. Old buildings are demolished to erect the modern city. While some laud what is new, others seek signs of what, in earlier times, had given their lives meaning— a familiar landmark, a childhood home. The nineteenth century, as the Romantic poets lamented, witnessed the replacement of an agrarian, rural life by an industrial city life. The twentieth century saw the emergence of the automobile and the television, liberating technologies in many ways but also ones that have stolen the outdoors and weakened public life. While the twenty-first century's powerful interactive media will also liberate and empower, new entailments will emerge to make disbelievers of some, alarmists of others.

The question of whether it is worth getting everyone online is also a Faustian bargain of sorts. Great striving and commitment will be required to meet the goals of a true Digital Nation, breaking the mold in the scope of society's commitment to provide entrée to skill building and knowledge for all. The body politic must be willing to show resolve over the long haul, and charismatic leadership is essential to show the way forward. Economies of scale and efficient delivery of service may also come at great cost unless attention is paid to preserving and expanding inclusion, providing the widest opportunity for everyone to migrate to cyberspace. The concentration of media owners[8] and a looming centralized surveillance society[9] are twin by-products of a society turned away from its civic responsibility and democratic aspirations. The question can be answered in many different ways but is largely viewed through two different lenses: the utilitarian one and the social justice perspective. These two worldviews often pass each other like ships in the night; they sometimes collide; but they can also sail together to create something more resilient than either's base elements. Former Speaker of the U.S. House of Representatives Thomas "Tip" O'Neill was fond of saying, Why make a moral argument when you can make an economic one? Based on years of experience in the U.S. Congress, O'Neill discerned when working with his colleagues that appealing to their enlightened self-interest was a more effective approach to achieving results than citing moral righteousness and social justice. This utilitarian approach may take various guises. The U.S. rejection of the Kyoto Accords on climate control, for example, hinged on a cost-benefit analysis, which U.S. decision makers used to find unacceptable the short-term costs imposed on U.S. businesses forced under the protocol to reduce their greenhouse gas emissions. Or it might take the form of logrolling, that is, trading votes for mutual gain,[10] for instance, an elected official from a rural agricultural area might trade a yes vote on a civil rights issue important to another official in exchange for a favorable vote on an agricultural tariff or subsidy bill. This approach's blind spot is to neglect equity concerns and a long-term view of the common interest for instrumental considerations.

The utilitarian approach has overrun policy deliberation, strengthened by the spread of economics and its obstinate striving to quantify alternative approaches to living, often stripped bare of ethical considerations.[11] In Helen Leavitt's fascinating account of the emergence of the interstate highway system, for example, she describes how cost-benefit analysis was used to justify the ceaseless expansion of what was originally planned as an effort to provide long-haul travel between cities and states. By midcentury the largest public works project ever undertaken had emerged, choking and obliterating neighborhoods and public spaces with thousands of miles of constructed highways. For Leavitt, the scheme's most egregious oversight was the disregard for human values in conceiving and implementing this plan as well as for a serious exploration of alternative modes of transportation. As she suggests, "No one has yet devised a method for putting a dollar value on space to live, work, play, and breathe."[12] Under the mantle of economic, security, and national defense arguments, the highway construction juggernaut continues and appears uncontrollable. In some of the country's most congested metropolitan areas, prominent planners and think tanks continue to peddle increased road building to accommodate an expanding economy.[13] The negative externalities of expansion are easy to identify yet hard to uproot, given that billions of dollars change hands to uphold entrenched commercial interests. Smart use of communications tools may be one provisional solution to begin to address the transportation bind. But unless they are part of a comprehensive, long-term solution, technological remedies will only serve to prolong our confrontation with the complex social and environmental challenges underlying our transportation woes.

A catalog of the tangible benefits of a Digital Nation surely needs to account for efficiency and productivity gains, but it must also include externalities and the possible unintended consequences of embedding these tools in everyday life. In the final analysis, a Digital Nation should be more just, not just more efficient. The well-documented automation of many occupations previously undertaken by white-collar or blue-collar workers, such as bank tellers or dockworkers, offers one constellation of efficiency gains with a dehumanizing effect on the unemployed[14] and consumers alike.[15] Occasionally the promise of gain, say, in internal business processes, is demonstrable, such as gains from Internet commerce or innovations in supply chain management. These efficiency gains may be a prelude to a more profound organizational transformation, or simply a red herring favoring the few at the expense of the many. The deregulation of broadcast industries in the name of efficiency, for example, has led to increased consolidation, further eroding the democratic potential of interactive communications.[16] While the proponents of deregulation promise innovation and investment as the fruits of government-induced competition, what has quickly materialized is monopoly's iron fist. Another example of a technology honeymoon turned sour is the invention of the moving assembly line. Developed in 1914 at Henry Ford's Highland Park, the incipient Fordist mode of production was originally hailed as a modern marvel but was soon used to intimidate workers, control them[17] and do them harm.[18] Faust's bargain turns to tragedy as the promise of creation turns to destruction without principles of generosity, reciprocity, and solidarity to counteract that of the acquisitive spirit.

The spread of economics and technological rationality has diminished the examination of issues from a social justice perspective. In chapter 4, I focus on the civil rights or social justice arguments for achieving a Digital Nation. In the end we must find a better balance between efficiency considerations and social justice as described by the late John Rawls in his classic, *A Theory of Justice*. For Rawls, demands for social justice should not necessarily conflict with the push for efficiency. The basic procedural arrangements of society in encouraging freedom and property protection will always create inequalities in the distribution of wealth and power. Without equity arrangements, society would resemble a poker match in which fair bets are placed among willing players, ultimately leading by dint of skill and luck to one player's winning the entire pot. Surely we would not consider this distribution just or fair as a function of pure procedural justice.[19] The backdrop for such procedural neutrality must be a just basic structure, a political constitution, and a fair arrangement of economic and social institutions. Fair economic opportunity and quality education are, of course, essential.

This system should also take into account redress and reciprocity as basic characteristics. A system of redress obliges society to give more attention to those born into less favorable social positions, so that redistributive policies attempt to alter the bias of contingencies and discrimination in the direction of equality. In a similar vein, what Rawls calls the difference principle works at a more general level to influence the total scheme of human arrangements, so that individuals favored by circumstance may gain from their good fortune only on terms improving the situation of losers. Whereas a policy of redress might target additional resources to intervene in poor children's early education, the difference principle operates to transform the aims of the basic structure (e.g., taxation), as Rawls suggests, so that it emphasizes more than social efficiency and technocratic values.[20]

Ultimately the difference principle expresses a conception of reciprocity in which human beings agree to share one another's fate; it evokes a sense of social solidarity, an attitude of mind and form of conduct animating a democratic ethos. Solidarity is difficult to maintain when stark inequalities exist between haves and have-nots. How are people at the bottom of the economic system to validate the position of those at the top when all they see is the bottom of the others' shoes? The social basis of self-respect is encouraged when the dignity of everyone's contribution to society is acknowledged, respected, and rewarded (e.g., addressing the perennial issue of low teacher pay in public education). Resources for education are to be allotted and justified not simply according to their return in productive abilities but also according to their worth in enriching the personal and social life of citizens, in building the social basis for self-respect and reciprocity.

Public support for universal education is an example of a productive melding of efficiency and social justice concerns. Support for public education is strong; its intrinsic value to a democratic order resonates deeply in the American psyche. The case for education's inherent value for society's well-being is embedded in shared values, woven into the country's warp and woof. While the public at large would be hard-pressed to point to specific figures or statistics as to the cost-benefit of public education, many favorable opinions are shaped by people's public education experience. An important subset of the public, parents, have a positive view of their children's schooling; communities support their local schools; and the public's support for education in general is palpable.

Data quantifying gains made in additional years of education offer strong support for the normative assumptions embodied in state constitutions and statutes that education is key to people's securing gainful employment and managing their own affairs. An examination of empirical trends suggests several clear developments. First, the future needs a more highly educated workforce. Data from the U.S. Department of Labor reveal that all but two of the fifty highest-paying occupations require a college degree. Air traffic controllers and nuclear power reactor operators are the only two of these jobs not requiring a college degree; however, they do demand extensive and long-term on-the-job training. What is more, the proportion of jobs calling for some postsecondary education has tripled between 1959 and today.[21] Second, climbing the educational ladder translates into higher salaries on the whole. In 1998 the mean lifetime earnings of males with an associate's degree were twice those of a high-school dropout.[22] Third, many salary differentials are growing, not shrinking, given the escalating requirements for higher education and skills in most growth industries. The jobs of bank teller, mortgage underwriter, or longshoreman may become obsolete, but somebody must build the machines and design the software to replace them. Last, education makes people more productive in managing their lives and honing skills. Governments in developing countries, for example, are expanding their investments in school construction, since evidence is mounting that schooling has positive labor market consequences.

The concept of human-capital formation suggests a healthy dynamic between the intrinsic and instrumental notion of education, one from which I borrow in making a case for a Digital Nation agenda. The human-capital approach situates the notion of the necessary skills the public education system must develop in the context of an overall theory of human development and democratic participation.[23] In a nutshell, this theory is animated by the belief that the formal and informal learning institutions with which we interact are central to achieving the freedom that is our inheritance. How can people be free in governing their lives and determining their futures, individually and collectively, without the fundamental skills and supportive learning environments to make mature and informed judgments? The term *human capital* evokes the idea of value emanating from the personal attributes or individual capacities one brings to the table. But the word *capital* also suggests that what is developed in terms of a person's skilled labor and intellectual capacity has an exchange value in the marketplaces of ideas and goods. National funding for education continues to rise in developed and developing nations, and the bar for mandatory education in developing nations, for example, is moving steadily from a baseline of primary education to requiring secondary school attendance, given education's positive role in building the economy.[24]

The dual rationale for education as an intrinsic and an instrumental good for a democratic society is similar to my argument for a Digital Nation agenda. Since telecommunications and media are critical enablers of anytime, anywhere learning, it is natural to see them enjoying a ride on the coattails of widespread support for education. Indeed, these are mutually reinforcing, since the public is independently sanguine about education and the potential of technology to improve people's lives. Mixing the two belief systems yields a powerful totem. A subset of education policy is educational technology, in which the cornerstone of national policymaking calls for universal provisioning of schools with modern communications, a policy the public widely supports.[25] In addition to hardware, professional development of teachers is viewed as critical; the public is aware of the hardships of the teaching profession and the low remuneration, so citizens are eager to provide the up-to-date tools and the training teachers need to succeed.

Of course, communications technology insinuates itself into more than education policy, becoming integral to e-health, social service transactions, and e-work. Rural health clinics, for example, are experimenting with e-health applications, and governments and private providers are realizing that home-based connectivity is an essential precondition for these promising practices. The public currently underwrites universal service through a line item appearing on people's monthly telephone bills, the Federal Universal Service Fund, a fee collected by industry and dispersed under the supervision of the Federal Communications Commission to subsidize the basic telecommunications needs of various households and public institutions. When the public is polled about the degree to which governments and industry should be contributing to building a Digital Nation, most people support an expanded role, even if it is not entirely clear what the benefits will be. A recent survey showed that 94 percent of adults support programs that make twenty-first century literacy a vital component in learning.[26] Harnessing the potential of digital television to meet public needs, not just providing entertainment, is something the public also values, such as obliging broadcasters to air more children's programming or public affairs shows.[27] Of course, it is another question altogether to explore what the public is willing to pay for prospective services, whether directly or indirectly, and it is unclear how these priorities stack up versus other domestic concerns. Depending on how questions are posed, education often rises to the top in polls asking respondents to rank foremost concerns. At other times and in other formats, concern for education is eclipsed by concerns about homeland security, economic viability, and health care. Doubtless how questions are asked, their timing, and the degree of leadership in shining a spotlight on them play important roles in positioning education and technology as national priority concerns. Integrating technology needs into perennial concerns for safety and economic development, for example, is key to sustaining a Digital Nation agenda. It is safe to say that in the right circumstances of political leadership—such as the Clinton White House's "digital opportunity" agenda in early 2000, backstopped by significant dollars, to implement "a comprehensive proposal to help bridge the digital divide and create new opportunity for all Americans"[28]—a Digital Nation agenda generates significant support and commitment across the political spectrum and in the public and private sectors.

Selling Bits instead of Atoms

The economic arguments for why decision makers in government and industry should accelerate their efforts to achieve universal digital literacy are persuasive. These arguments hit us all in our wallets and purses, and I review what we know about the economic benefits of migrating the nation and its residents toward high performance with smart use of information tools. Amazon.com highlights the efficiency of a centralized distribution system and an e-commerce model over and against one in which consumers physically transport themselves to a retail store—the latter, in the aggregate, contributing to air pollution, traffic congestion, fossil fuel demand, and landfill waste. As long as we cross-check the gains made through the productive use of new technologies with Rawls's difference principle, ensuring that new investments contribute to social equality, we can begin to appraise realistically the net payoffs of building a Digital Nation.

The positive effects of information technology diffusion impact all sectors of economic, educational, and civic life; they add fuel to the argument that concerted efforts today to continue scaling high-performance programs will yield striking dividends in outlying years. A thumbnail portrait of how various industries are making strides through investments in communications technologies illustrates what a Digital Nation might resemble. In agriculture, for example, managing the volatility of the marketplace is a risky proposition. Yet with digital technologies, North Dakota farmers and ranchers, constituting 38 percent of the state's economic base, are competing in a global marketplace, employing creative risk management strategies through networking and timely access to information over the Internet. Examples abound from the developing world in which farmers are using the Internet to bypass expensive middlemen and taking their products directly to global markets. With health care annual expenditures totaling $1.2 trillion, or 13 percent of the national Gross Domestic Product, physicians are using smart technologies for home monitoring, allowing digital transmission of patients' vital statistics, thereby reducing cost, extending access, and enhancing outpatient services.[29] Intelligent systems have also improved the surface transportation network immensely,[30] and new traffic alleviation strategies in Finland rely on signals from drivers' mobile telephones to gauge congestion and to warn fellow commuters.

E-work and e-commerce also bode well for future energy efficiency, with the movement of bits instead of atoms generally resulting in fewer environmental effects.[31] Decision makers hail the productivity gains that information technologies enable in the private sector, eager to duplicate them in promoting e-government and e-learning. Thirty percent of economic growth between 1996 and 2000 is attributable to the information technology sector, according to one account.[32] Given these dramatic changes, one might plausibly wonder why the nation is not deepening its investments in high-performance programs, accelerating the pace of innovation to refresh economic and social life.

With industries in transformation, or in need of transformation, a heightened threshold of literacy is required to navigate and succeed in a world with fewer gatekeepers. People trading stocks or buying homes need sharper financial and technical literacy, particularly if they are cutting out intermediaries in these transactions to save money: information and communications technologies have made this "disintermediation" possible. With some industries, such as residential real estate, a huge potential exists for the public to benefit from the application of Internet-based technologies. With U.S. homeownership near record levels, with about seven out of ten households paying a mortgage, the money paid to realtors, lawyers, title companies, and lenders adds up to tens of billions of dollars annually. Cutting into this industry from a consumer perspective—and from the vantage of applying technology to end-run gatekeepers—will require sharp information literacy and technology skills as well as changes in laws to loosen the information stranglehold from entrenched interests, such as the real estate lobby. Having and applying new literacy skills could make the difference between owning a home or not for thousands of Americans who otherwise cannot afford the high costs associated with traditional home buying. An in-depth look at e-health and e-work illustrates the benefits of forging a Digital Nation.

Stemming the Health Care Crisis

Many observers believe that information and communications technologies have enormous potential to enable or improve health and health care, containing cost, enhancing quality, and extending access. The term *e-health* is used as a catchall for a variety of health sector applications—

everything from telemedicine, the use of telecommunications to provide medical information and services, to medical informatics, the collection and distribution of data such as computer-based medical records. While these practices may sound arcane, they hold real promise in bringing more comprehensive, real-time health service to more people at a lower cost than traditional health care offerings. Real-time diagnosis and treatment cannot be underestimated. In a rural community where specialists are often in short supply, accurate diagnosis and rapid treatment might mean the difference between life and death. At a recent hearing before the House Committee on Agriculture to review the U.S. Department of Agriculture's Distance Learning and Telemedicine Program, the Under-Secretary for Rural Development, Thomas Dorr, relayed the story of Dheva Muthurama-lingam, born two days shy of the millennium in a small community hospital in West Virginia. Plagued by respiratory problems and a heart murmur, Dheva was transferred to the Winchester Medical Center for diagnosis by an adult cardiologist. The doctor determined the baby had a hole in his heart and also exhibited other symptoms requiring further diagnosis. Fortunately, a specialist at the University of Virginia's Medical Center two hours away reviewed Dheva's heart ultrasound transmitted via a telemedicine connection, diagnosed a rare congenital heart defect, and prescribed immediate medical treatment to stabilize the infant for safe transport. The doctors involved in Dheva's case believed he might have been misdiagnosed or not have survived the trip to Charlottesville if the prior remote diagnosis had not been made.[33]

Examples of e-health date from the late 1950s, with doctors in Nebraska performing telepsychiatry and medical professionals doing teleradiology in Montreal, Canada. Notwithstanding such early successes, e-health did not take off as a mainstream medical practice until the mid-1990s. The Association of Telehealth Service Providers, the trade association for the telehealth industry, acknowledged only three telemedicine programs operating in North America in 1991, a figure growing to 206 ten years later.[34] What accounts for the long dormancy in e-health activity and the skyrocketing activity in the late 1990s? The short answer relates to the acceptability of these unorthodox practices within the cultural milieu and established models of the medical profession. In order for e-health to migrate from alternative practice to the mainstream, the entire apparatus of medicine had to become more nimble, reforming professional training, licensing, reimbursement, and generally the financial, legal, and professional codes defining acceptable practice.

Surely, the information and technology revolution of the 1990s created fertile ground for experimentation in the health care arena. Innovations in the financial and manufacturing sectors as well as the spread of e-commerce had an important effect, witnessed in the growth of informatics and the deepening of service delivery via telecommunications or Internet-based systems. The growing acceptability of these tools on the part of businesses and customers—and the availability of large investment dollars to underwrite new entrepreneurship—contributed to the rapid growth of e-health applications in the second half of the 1990s. Success breeds success and enhances the acceptability of e-health to a broader professional cohort.

Spiraling health care expenditures represent another impetus for new cost containment strategies. With health care costs doubling from $1.1 trillion in 1998 to a projected $2.2 trillion in 2008 (16 percent of GDP), many experts see a major role for information and communications technologies in reducing transaction costs. About a quarter of health care expenditures can be attributed to administrative inefficiencies and waste.[35] The U.S. Department of Health and Human Services has an incentive to promote more widespread adoption of telemedicine, given that 81 percent of its half-a-trillion-dollar-plus budget outlay feeds Medicare and Medicaid-related expenditures. In a lengthy 2001 report to Congress, however, department staff dedicated only one-and-a-half pages to documenting telecommunications and Internet-based cost-saving measures. Clearly, the federal government must also more robustly sponsor research and experimentation in e-health to populate the public record with evidence that one day may lead to practices affecting the overall health care budget.

One author has approached cost savings in e-health in terms of "four Cs": connectivity, content, commerce, and care.[36] The components are considered separately to scrutinize the potential to gain health care efficiencies; however, an effective remedy would likely contain all these elements in a single integrated approach. The informaticization of medical records, claims processing, and the like may significantly reduce the transaction costs of administrative and clinical functions. Since managed care organizations estimate administrative costs at approximately 15 percent of total spending, electronic or Web-based data interchanges processed at a fraction of the cost of paper claims may begin to make inroads in total administrative expenses as use increases. Only about 7 percent of U.S. physicians use electronic medical records, for example; but using electronic medical records systems simply to reduce paper chart pulls and transcription costs would yield a net financial benefit of $18,200 per primary care provider, according to a recent study published in the *American Journal of Medicine.*[37]

In terms of content—the second of the four Cs—millions of people are now scouring the Internet for health-related information, surfing health care portals, such as WebMD, to enhance wellness. If information-seeking behavior were perfect, then people would absorb as much information as possible to make a maximally rational choice. These choices would then likely lead to potentially beneficial life choices involving better prevention, more accurate diagnosis, or stronger treatment. Yet a cost-benefit model akin to Anthony Downs's theory of rational choice[38] posits people as psychologically making reasonable choices based on satisfying their information needs,[39] often aligned with preexisting frames of reference. Indigent children have a higher likelihood of suffering poor oral health, and public health messages have generally been ineffective because adults, who make decisions about their children's oral hygiene and eating habits, for example, are caught up in a mass consumer society promoting fast foods and unhealthy lifestyles. Promoting media literacy to analyze critically and filter misleading content and "open access" for publicly funded medical research[40] are fundamental to parlaying health-related content into positive outcomes for individuals and society.

Electronic commercial transactions (the third "C"), business-to-business and business-to-consumer, represent another significant financial masterstroke to streamline service delivery. Robert Litan and Alice Rivlin have painstakingly analyzed the benefits of an enhanced information economy:

Much of the contribution of the Internet to productivity growth will arise not from new activities, but simply from faster, cheaper handling of information needed in ordinary business transactions, such as ordering, billing, and getting information to employees, suppliers, and customers. Information–intensive sectors, such as financial services, health services, and government are likely to see their transactions costs cut substantially.[41]

Just to offer one example of the promise of business-to-business commerce, the total processing costs of supplying health care supplies are about $23 billion, including inventory management. One study estimates that 49 percent of the processing costs could be eliminated through efficient product movement, information sharing, and order management.[42]

The last of the four Cs, care, relates to the promising use of information and communications technologies to improve health care. Both access to and the quality of health care are being improved by innovative telehealth applications. In terms of the quality of health care, telemedicine can be an effective tool in increasing the responsiveness, depth, and evenness of care. Anecdotal evidence from an evaluation report of a telehospice program in Michigan and Kansas described the case of a caregiver who called the extended coverage team at 3 a.m. to report that the hospice patient was in severe abdominal pain. The on-call nurse was sixty miles away from the patient's rural residence, so the nurse asked the caregiver to pan the telehospice unit (basically videophone equipment) over the patient's body to pinpoint the problem. Seeing that the patient's catheter tube was kinked, obstructing the flow of urine, the nurse instructed the caregiver to straighten the catheter, providing rapid response while also saving the nurse two hours' driving.[43]

Another example from the Hays Medical Center's telemedicine department in Hays, Kansas, reveals that shorter hospital stays (lowered by 15 percent since 1972, with outpatient visits nearly doubling) confront attending physicians with acute challenges in monitoring and receiving important feedback on discharged patients' vital statistics. Using existing phone lines to transmit data, a newly developed technology automatically allows monitoring nurses to receive, in digital form, the patient's blood pressure, blood oxygen, weight, temperature, blood glucose, and heart rate measures. An independent evaluation showed that using technology for home monitoring results in better health and a sense of well-being among patients at a vulnerable stage in their recovery.[44]

In terms of expanding access to health care (for example, to those who live too far from a medical facility or to some of the 42 million uninsured or underinsured persons), technology offers a way to broaden affordable, efficient health care service to residents outside the bounds of the health care system. In Washington County, Maine, the easternmost county in the United States, one can begin to picture the benefits of e-health. The nearest hospital and medical specialist are two to three hours away, in Bangor, Maine. Joyce F. lives by herself in Calais, Maine; she is elderly and suffers from diabetes and first-stage Alzheimer's disease. To ensure that she takes her medicine, Joyce visits with a nurse daily through a videoconferencing device that sits unobtrusively in her living room, connected to a regular phone line and featuring a postcard-size color monitor.[45]

Another example of e-health's reaching into the ranks of the uninsured is the University of Virginia telemedicine program. Begun in 1995 and supported in part by federal dollars, the program networks over forty hospitals, clinics, prisons, and schools in poor rural parts of the state, providing affordable and enhanced access to health professionals with twenty-five different subspecialties. Since the indigent and the uninsured cannot afford medical service, particularly labs, X-rays, and the like, the program discounts the patient's charges based on family income and size, to as low as five dollars per visit. Over one-half of patients at the Saltville Medical Center, four hours from the University of Virginia hospital, are uninsured. Providing quality access to specialty care to underserved communities would simply not be possible without an affordable e-health program, a hub-and-spoke system connecting the entire region to clinicians otherwise unavailable to meet poor people's health needs.

Unclogging the Autobahn

Americans drive more than 2.6 trillion miles a year, with increasing demand for transportation now reaching the limits of capacity in some regions. In the past two decades, traffic congestion has worsened, both for small and large metropolitan areas. In a study of seventy-five urban areas across the country, the Texas Transportation Institute found that commuting times during rush hours grew by 25 percent between 1982 and 2000.[46] On average, a traveler spends an extra 62 hours per year delayed in peaktime congestion, a figure ranging from 136 hours in Los Angeles (imagine, five-and-a-half days per year sitting in traffic!) to two days per year in Pensacola, Florida, a relatively small urban area.[47] In the largest cities, commuters now expect to spend over an hour a day commuting to and from work, and soaring housing costs sometimes push working families hours from their employers.[48]

The cost of traffic congestion in lost productivity and fuel consumption is enormous. The value of time and energy wasted in gridlock traffic amounts to a staggering $67.5 billion for the seventy-five urban areas surveyed in the Texas Transportation Institute study, roughly equal to the

Gross Domestic Product of Chile or New Zealand.[49] Relieving a single traveler from rush-hour congestion would save over $1,000 per commuter, a figure that should begin to motivate citizen groups and businesses to press for concerted action in reducing congestion. Greater than individual inconvenience is the idea of marginal congestion: my driving to work makes others' commutes slightly worse because I become an obstacle in the free flow of traffic. According to Paul Krugman, a Princeton professor, each individual's decision to commute by car in Atlanta imposes a cost of $3,500 per year on other people, costs over and above those actually paid by the driver in lost productivity and fossil fuels.[50]

Strategies to alleviate congestion can come in various guises: adding surface capacity, managing demand, or expanding travel options. Building more roads will of course continue, but public debate rages over whether the pace of road building will actually displace demand, not to mention concern over the environmental and social costs of expanding surface road construction. Instituting time-shifting options is promising, transitioning the culture of work away from reliance on a nine-to-five rhythm. Managing demand, including ride sharing, congestion pricing, and teletravel, tends to be less politically acceptable but ultimately has broader effects than supply-side remedies, such as building more roads.[51]

Two noted economists, Robert Crandall and Charles Jackson, have quantified the potential financial savings from e-work, based on fairly widespread adoption of telecommuting and appropriate business and government incentives. Assuming 30 percent of jobs nationally allow telecommuting one day per week (the average commute for a teleworker is 20 minutes), the authors were able to calculate the potential savings in travel time and congestion costs at $23 billion annually.[52] These figures are not too far-fetched because 10–20 percent of workers currently telecommute at least part-time,[53] a number that could double by 2005, according to the International Telework Association and Council.

Those who stay off the roads and telecommute benefit society in various ways, including lowering individual and marginal congestion costs and alleviating pollution. Employers, not just employees, also gain from appropriate implementation of e-work. Having fewer employees on site translates into lower overhead costs and generally increases productivity, according to the Canadian Telework Association, resulting in thousands of dollars in savings per worker annually. IBM reaps benefits in allowing about 25 percent of its global workforce to work remotely, for example, saving over $2,000 in yearly real estate costs. An independent evaluation of a telecommuting project in Los Angeles found annual economic benefits of $6,100 per worker.[54] Such benefits are striking, but they do not serve as a sufficient strategy for addressing transportation challenges.

From the Crystal Palace to Silicon Valley

The wealth creation and entrepreneurial buzz surrounding places such as Seattle and Silicon Valley export a philosophy in which the full potential of high technology markets has yet to be unleashed to solve pressing social problems. Home to the world's largest corporations, largest private foundations, and most active coterie of Internet venture capitalists, these epicenters of technological prowess innovate and develop new products and applications, with the research and development budget of Microsoft larger than the total product of most developing countries. The worldview and energy typified in these regions, even after the dot-com implosion, give rise to a fervent belief that the business potential of information and communications technologies is so immense that, if fully realized, it could alleviate social distress, poverty, illiteracy, and underdevelopment worldwide. The examples of cost savings from e-health and e-work, if taken to the extreme, would reinforce the ideology in which the deepening of technology investment alone would solve health care and transportation problems. If the proper market-friendly environment is cultivated in societies across the globe, so goes the argument, we will witness the mitigation of poverty, illiteracy, and disease in this generation while at the same time making a small pocket of individuals very wealthy.

Such a vision extends a long legacy of euphoric speculation about the effects of unfettered markets and technological advances on human progress. At the time of the erection of the famous Crystal Palace for the Great Exhibition of 1851, the prevailing wisdom was that the relaxation of tariffs and other barriers to trade would usher in a period of prosperity without end. The construction of the breathtaking edifice was meant to be a beacon for progress, showcasing the artifacts of international commerce and trade while displaying the latest conveniences, such as the indoor water closet.[55] Alfred, Lord Tennyson wrote a poem to honor the event, called "Ode Sung at the Opening of the International Exhibition," in which he likened "growing Commerce" to "the fair white-wing'd peacemaker" that will bring nations together and strengthen social solidarity.[56] The similarities between Tennyson's optimism and euphoric pronouncements about new information and communications technologies as lubricants for international trade remind us that there is a common thread embedded in Enlightenment thinking[57] over the past several hundred years: unfortunately, the idea of human improvement has fused with commodity exchange, such that "the culture industry has taken over the civilizing inheritance of the entrepreneurial and frontier democracy."[58]

The Crystal Palace was a harbinger of the consumer society, serving as the prototype for what would become the twentieth-century shopping mall. Invented in the mid-nineteenth century in London and Paris, and made possible by innovations in glass-and-steel construction, the arcade or department store architecture originally produced beautiful glass-enclosed shopping arenas that enhanced the packaging and display of commodities and the social experience of window-shopping.[59] Over the past century and a half the cinematic shopping experience has thrived and the culture industry has become ubiquitous. Seeing and being seen in enclosed spaces, usually ones in recent years to which consumers must drive, are part and parcel of what passes today for public life. With communications technologies and the domestication of electronic shopping, commodity exchange is becoming virtual. When viewed through the lens of efficiency, there is no process more sanitized and efficient than virtual window-shopping. Particularly if one lives a busy life, navigating congested urban and suburban communities where traffic and incivility are mounting, and terrorism and communicable diseases loom, what safer solution exists than online shopping? Or, for that matter, one can undertake a range of activities, including schooling and medical diagnosis, without leaving one's house.

As has been detailed, these innovations liberate and empower in many ways. But they also portend new cultural norms with unknown consequences for what passes today for democratic life. They also may be poor substitutes for other policy remedies that offer more durable solutions to social ills. For example, while e-health will extend health care to uninsured people, it will likely not replace the need to build new clinics in rural communities, to attract specialists and other professionals into remote areas, and to devise strategies to insure a greater number of low-income persons.

Developing long-term policy solutions to many social challenges will in many instances integrate effective uses of information and communications technologies; yet efficiency gains alone will be a poor yardstick to gauge overall human betterment.

It is not too much of a stretch to extend the logic of digitization toward seeing people as expendable, even disposable. The history of automation suggests that some people will exploit others to make money. And the grueling circumstances of early automation continue in many parts of the world, including in our own backyards. Two of the greatest nineteenth-century political theorists, John Stuart Mill and Karl Marx, both saw in automation and technological advancement the chance to liberate humanity from drudgery and what Marx called the "realm of necessity."[60] Greater productivity would curtail labor time and reduce energy expenditure, giving human workers the potential of leading fulfilling lives outside of work. For Marx and Mill alike, much depended on the just distribution of the fruits of this productive process and a high degree of social solidarity and reciprocity, attributes that are in short supply with wealth and the traffic of information and ideas concentrated in the hands of a few.

4

The New Frontier of Civil Rights

A notorious symbol of de jure segregation, a steel drinking fountain with the words "whites only" on it has become an indelible image of the struggle and hardship many Americans endured in the era prior to the gains of the civil rights movement of the 1960s. Segregationist and discriminatory practices created a color bar in which access to good jobs, a sound education, and the voting booth were severely curtailed. These practices have created lasting seams in our social fabric, gaps in skills and earnings that arrest economic and community development in many parts of the country.

Imagine an equally exclusionary society in which success depends on the effective navigation of digital media, if etched over university halls or voting booths or places of employment were the words "digital only," a prescription that only those with digital mastery may enter. The history of broadcast ownership in the second half of the twentieth century was a history of discrimination against minorities,[1] contributing in part to abysmally low broadcast ownership rates among people of color as well as the stereotypical and demeaning portrayal of ethnic and racial groups generally in the media.[2] If we look at entry barriers to the knowledge society, then clearly there are millions without the skills or credentials to participate meaningfully. As technology begins to improve people's lives, it is no surprise that communities without access to and ownership of these tools are raising their voices to be heard. Communities struggling with substandard educational facilities, chronic underemployment, and alienation from unresponsive political systems are particularly concerned to devise the right strategies to gain entry to digital opportunities on a nondiscriminatory basis.

At the same time that communities are struggling to exercise their freedoms to participate meaningfully in the digital age, governments and commercial forces are marshaling these tools to surveil and profile the public in pernicious ways. Some leaders have referred to this century as the battleground for a new civil rights struggle—that of control over the manipulation of information, communications, and technology. Some see the twenty-first-century battlefield, from the international relations perspective, as literally a struggle to dampen the communications fields of one's opponent. And news outlets have tirelessly documented Al Qaeda's use of mobile communications to sustain and nourish its virtual terror network. On the domestic front, the U.S. government is building a vast data warehouse to monitor data transaction and movement. So the euphoria of the early 1990s, of government's role as catalyst in the development of a decentralized, democratic medium, has been displaced in part by a dystopian vision in which the government is spending vast resources to erect the twenty-first-century equivalent of the panopticon. The Defense Advanced Research Projects Agency (DARPA), the same agency that developed the Internet, is now developing the Terrorism Information Awareness program, a surveillance plan to predict patterns of movement and action through an examination of people's data remains.[3]

In its zeal to defend the homeland, the government is thwarting its own logic, as outlined in its security documents, that the surest way to nurture security at home is to promote literacy and learning.[4] In a world in which one-half of the population is under 25, and 80 percent of these youths live in poverty, it is imperative that young people find meaningful work and can plug into the global marketplace of commerce and ideas, lest seeds of discontent spread. This is no less true at home than in the developing world. Yet communities of color and poor Americans are doubly the losers in the drive to control information: as the victims of surveillance and racial profiling and the losers in a budget battle where social programs are starved to feed the voracious defense and homeland security budgets.

National leadership in the United States is lagging in articulating a vision for what it means to be a full participant in a Digital Nation where media and communications tools can be harnessed to empower people, to improve their health and expand their earning potential. The European Union launched the eEurope initiative and action plan. At the national level, the Office of the e-Envoy was established to get the United Kingdom online and to use information and communications tools to improve people's lives.[5] The e-Envoy possesses the authority to convey why mastery of these technologies is important and how equitable access will be achieved. This level of transparency is essential to achieve a Digital Nation so that elected leaders can be held accountable for their policies and proposals in moving countries forward.

Articulating this vision might take the form of a bill of rights for a Digital Nation, one that reflects the potential of these tools to empower, educate, and inspire. The ideal vision of media and communications in a democracy is one in which everyone can find multiple entryways into cyberspace on a nondiscriminatory basis, predicated on the availability of opportunities to develop the capacity to use these tools and, at the same time, to have one's civil liberties protected. So the positive vision of cyberspace and interactive media is critical, as captured in a document such as the Universal Declaration of Human Rights, which asserts not only a right to "freedom of opinion and expression" but also a right "to seek, receive and impart information and ideas through any media and regardless of frontiers."[6]

Because a national framework eludes us, social justice advocates have had to hitch their technology equity agenda onto preexisting frameworks, reinterpreting and updating seminal civil rights touchstones such as *Brown v. Board of Education,* the Civil Rights Act, and the Voting Rights Act. New arguments are being shaped articulating how schools today require technology to deliver an up-to-date education. And with the way Internet voting and the electronic delivery of government services have been bandied about, concerns about digital disenfranchisement have been raised. This chapter looks broadly at judicial remedies to address digital equity and to usher in a Digital Nation, focusing on the obligations of public education and governments to serve all peoples without discrimination.

An Up-to-Date Education for All

Some say that creating the environment for a sound education in the digital age requires dismantling the nineteenth-century schoolhouse and replacing it with a learning environment that melds the potential of educational technologies with the growing knowledge of the diverse ways in which human beings interact and learn. By any standard, many schools in some of our largest urban centers are irreparably broken and need radical surgery, not Band-Aids, to ensure that students can achieve.

Lawsuits have been brought against state governments in all but five states for providing substandard education to children of color and those living in poverty.[7] In some instances, the financial resources are inadequate to achieve a threshold level of quality, in human capital and equipment, including attracting seasoned teachers. The inadequacy of resources, equipment, and services is to a certain extent a moving target because technological change and social context make one-size-fits-all solutions difficult to prescribe. This said, social justice advocates today are looking less at incremental change to shore up a broken system and more at reforming failed schools from the ground up. Seen from the vantage point of what constitutes full participation in the twenty-first-century economy and civil society, school reform takes on a different hue. And the argument for equity takes on a more urgent overtone: how to revive a failing school system so that an entire cohort of kids can be contributors to the economy and society, one that will rely more heavily on facility with technology, sharp cognitive skills, and the sound interpretation of media messages.

In short, the right to receive a sound basic or adequate education in the twenty-first century means discarding outmoded notions of education and positing the underachieving urban student in a state-of-the-art, nimble learning environment, supported by well-trained teachers, relevant curriculum, and modern information and communications tools. Rather than bypassing an entire cohort of young people at risk of dropping out, an opportunity exists, made possible by communications technologies, to bypass the institutions that fail young people. Historic defenders of public education, groups such as the National Urban League, have recently thrown down the gauntlet, challenging behemoth, out-of-date, anonymous schools to reform or be replaced by small state-of-the-art schools focused on learning. Every child, regardless of his or her income or race, requires greater educational opportunities to be equipped for equal citizenship and economic self-reliance in the twenty-first century.

My own experience in examining school equity from the viewpoint of the enabling role technology can play in enhancing teaching and learning is colored by an encounter I had as a researcher in the mid-1990s. At that time, I was evaluating an east Texas school district's ability to integrate technology into learning at a time when public and private technology programs were throwing technology at schools. On one of my tours through a school, inevitably my interviews took me to the school library, where I wanted to see not only whether it had entered the computer age, with student-accessible terminals, but also the state of the book collections.

Upon entering the small, spartan library, I almost stumbled over a large box, on the side of which was pictured a high-end Apple computer. Three of these unopened boxes blocked my path to a row of shelves on which rested tattered books and well-worn, slightly out-of-date magazines.

My interview with the librarian was a short one. She was an older woman and had taught at the school for many years. When I asked her about the influx of computers and the connections that would be made to the latest artery of communications, the Internet, she was not at all heartened. While she did not deride the new order per se, she talked with hesitation, skeptical about technology matters. She said she was retiring and signaled that she would leave her kingdom to younger mavens. The truth emerged upon further investigation that these computers had been dropped off in her and other teachers' classrooms without their full knowledge or consent. Little thought had been given to the fact that many teachers at that time had never or only rarely used a computer and that their attitudes to the new technology ranged from trepidation to hostility, as if their tried-and-true teaching methods were somehow under assault. Very little professional development in integrating technology into classroom instruction had taken place over the summer to develop teachers' skills. The general sentiment was that they would adapt and that their classrooms would never be the same again.

One of the many ironies with this technology windfall is that the fund established to wire these schools, the Telecommunications Infrastructure Fund,[8] emerged from talks between Texas state officials and the local telephone monopoly, SBC Communications, over loosening the regulatory strictures under which the company operated. In exchange for higher profits and greater market share, the community benefited from the $10 billion largesse, bumping up the state from the near bottom in terms of computer penetration and Internet connectivity. While shareholders saw their dividend checks grow, schools, amidst already harrowing circumstances, were experiencing at first hand what happens when technology outpaces the ability to control and manipulate it effectively.

The lesson here is that any discussion of technology's role in education, as important as I think it is, should not be first and foremost about getting more hardware and tools into classrooms. Unfortunately, most of the policies during the 1990s (and continuing today) were focused on hardware solutions, either as a settlement in consumer action against malfeasant telecommunications, computer, and media companies (Toshiba is among the latest examples here) or as government policy to provide a dividend to the public in exchange for regulatory forbearance. What resulted was an imbalance in which 95 cents of every dollar is spent on hardware, when the ratio should be closer to 50–70 cents on the dollar.

As statistics show, even with these massive public and private investments (tens of billions of dollars), the distribution of multimedia computers and Internet connections still favors affluent schools and communities. But this should not be the main focus of civil rights leaders and advocates as they articulate what constitute adequate facilities in the digital age. Indeed, the opportunity exists to rethink radically so that technology enhancement will not be just one more concession added to the list but rather an invitation to rethink how education is delivered, particularly to students with special circumstances and unique learning needs.

Two strategies have been put into effect to equalize resources in school districts. First, state action (in New Jersey) to redress imbalances in district funding resulting from property tax allocations has had a salutary effect. And the federal government has simultaneously sought to provide funds to communities with a high incidence of poverty and also to rural, isolated communities.

But the challenge to states and school districts has been not only to achieve financial equity but also equity in the opportunities, facilities, and resources to learn. For example, achieving parity for the first time through school finance restructuring is a critical step but does not lead straightforwardly to a closing of the skills and achievement gaps. Schools and districts may be so far behind because of neglect and underresourcing that they may be unable to operate at the levels at which other schools, with experienced teachers and more nurturing learning environments, perform. We know, for example, that the most experienced teachers do not gravitate to the most challenged schools; indeed, the opposite is true. So, incentives are required to cajole seasoned teachers to take on the challenge of schooling at-risk young people, often in harrowing circumstances.

Underserved districts are looking for ways to steadily enhance student performance, and technology provides an invitation to engage young people. However, with the passage of the "No Child Left Behind" legislation,[10] underperforming districts are under enormous pressure to focus on raising standardized test performance, a process that will likely alienate already struggling kids (perhaps pushing them out of the schoolhouse door) than attract them to the learning process.

Lawsuits have focused on achieving financial parity as well as on providing "opportunities to learn." Even when opportunities become available, in the form of categorical grants from public and private sources, under-resourced schools do not always have the capacity to respond. So E-rate dollars (see chapter 5), aimed at the worst-off schools and libraries, have not always gone to them. For example, many schools in impoverished parts of the country, such as the Mississippi Delta, have not availed themselves of many of the technology discount opportunities because they lack the personnel to pull together the applications. With federal legislation shining a spotlight on underperforming schools, there is an impetus to change; yet, without the resources to effect change, how can these schools make progress?

With the provision to ensure that all eighth-graders become technology-literate, states are beginning to create standards, curricula, and diagnostics to gauge their performance. This, again, amounts to an unfunded mandate, particularly as the definition expands to include a host of skills necessary to compete in the twenty-first century, such as cognitive and civic skills. Technical skills will be hard enough to come by as funding is slashed for technology at the federal and state levels, because poor kids still have scant access to technology in their homes and schools. Often, in distressed communities, computer labs are locked up to avoid theft or are in various states of disrepair because of lack of user support. Sometimes new computers sit in unopened boxes because teachers may lack the interest, training, or know-how to set up and use the new learning tools.

Most state constitutions guarantee some form of basic or adequate education, and policymakers and educators link the necessary components of this education to preparing young people for gainful employment and the obligations of citizenship. By examining what the modern economy and civic duty demand, one can articulate plausible expectations for young people in terms of the cognitive and technical skills required to be ready for these realities. A growing consensus is emerging about the relative weight of technology literacy in being prepared for a knowledge economy, as evidenced by the national provisioning of technology literacy by eighth grade as well as by the adoption of state requirements for technology professional development for teachers in twelve states.[11] With the widespread educational failure to deliver these basic facilities and instructional materials, parents and concerned citizens are appealing to state courts to ameliorate the woefully outdated state of education facing underserved young people and communities of color.

Perhaps the most high-profile suit currently is that of the Campaign for Fiscal Equity, Inc., against the state of New York in the case of New York City's public schools. Under way for the better part of a decade, the lawsuit challenges the state to furnish adequate resources to provide students with the opportunities to achieve and the system the ability to educate its students. The record of failure in the city is notorious, with up to 40 percent of students who enter the ninth grade not completing high school, a statistic rivaled by many other large city school districts. Fully one-third of the system's elementary students are illiterate. On the basis of these failures, the trial court in Albany deemed that an unacceptable number of students were leaving school unprepared for a life of gainful employment, higher education, and the duties incumbent on democratic citizenship.

An emergent constitutional standard might reasonably expect students to obtain a high school degree, a threshold for gainful employment today, as well as the fundamental cognitive, technical, and communicative skills to meet the demands of a modern economy. It is a given for most business leaders and a growing body of educators that students be technologically adept and that preparedness for the modern workforce requires technology skills as requisite, not supplemental. The weight of evidence provided at the trial revealed that New York City public schools have failed for over a decade to provide adequate instructional technology to students, measured both in terms of quantity and quality of hardware, peripherals, and software. What is worse, the building infrastructure is often too obsolete to provide adequate electric power and telecommunications to support computers and Internet connectivity.

The voice of the voiceless is being heard throughout the nation as state after state is brought to account for its failure to deliver an adequate, sound education to its neediest students. On the West Coast, the case *Williams v. the State of California* has challenged the appalling conditions many children face across California, from unqualified teachers to poor ventilation and air-conditioning. In the state that spawned Silicon Valley, many students remain excluded from the information economy, unable to gain computer skills or use the Internet to conduct research. While advocates continue to battle for a quality education for all students, regardless of economic background and color, educational technologies can play a significant role in transforming teaching and learning for underserved communities. In chapter 5, I explore some inspiring examples of school districts undergoing a metamorphosis because of fiscal parity, visionary leadership with high expectations, innovative pedagogies, and an infusion of computing and communications tools to connect stakeholders responsible for learning success.

Voting Made Easy . . . for Some

In March 2000 a seemingly salutary alteration of the voting process occurred in Arizona and was met with great fanfare, an event that largely fell under the radar screen of the national media. To the extent that it was covered at all, it was embraced gleefully as a sign of forward progress in the age-old desire to fold everyone into the democratic process. This event was Internet voting. Fueled by money from the for-profit Internet company Election.com, the Arizona Democratic party hosted the first-ever binding online vote. Registered Democrats across the state were given four days to vote in the primary. However, citizens' primary mechanism for participating during the three days leading up to the March 11 primary was remote Internet voting. On the fourth day, the Democratic electorate could vote only at polling stations, using either traditional paper ballots or special Internet workstations.

Prior to the election, registered Arizona Democrats received a PIN number in the mail to be used for online voting and information regarding mail-in ballots. A second follow-up mailing alerted voters to the 114 public online polling sites. Voters who chose to participate online at the public sites or their own computers could do so from Tuesday, March 7, until 11:59 p.m. on Friday, March 10, the day prior to the primary. Those who opted to vote using the traditional paper ballot had to do so between 10 a.m. and 7 p.m. on primary day (March 11) or via a mail-in ballot.

Internet voting represents a new approach to the ballot that, if implemented appropriately, promises to increase the efficiency and reliability of elections. At a time when the dot-com excitement was at a fever pitch, Internet companies, buoyed by venture capital funding, were able to test their proof of concept with abandon. From the company's point of view, success with the prototype would cement its brand as a trusted early entrant into a market in which demand for online services seemed to be rising geometrically. Given that the Arizona Democratic party's 2000 presidential preference primary was the first binding election in which online voting was permitted, much was riding on the success of this venture. From the Democratic party's point of view, this novel approach was meant to reinvigorate the political process, greatly expanding turnout among registered Democrats, including minorities. Most registered voters stay home in primary elections, particularly when little is at stake. With online voting, registered voters with a connection to the Internet could literally stay home and still register their preferences.

While the new procedure on its face might appear innocuous, the context of rolling it out in Arizona raised the eyebrows of civil libertarians. In February 2000 a nonprofit organization based in northern Virginia, the Voter Integrity Project, filed a complaint against the Arizona Democratic party and its chairman, Mark Fleisher, seeking a preliminary injunction to enjoin the Internet voting portion of the election under section 2 of the Voting Rights Act. The Voter Integrity Project and four registered Democrats, two African-American and two Hispanic, claimed that the effect of Internet voting would be to maximize white electoral participation at the expense of ethnic and racial minorities. The argument went that as a class, African-Americans, Native Americans, and Hispanics would have less opportunity to exercise their franchise than other members of the electorate, given the reality of the digital divide, that is, the disparate access to computers and the Internet that exists in Arizona. The case hinged on an interpretation of section 2 of the Voting Rights Act, an acknowledgment of the stark digital divide that exists in the state, and a belief that the consequences of such a divide would be detrimental to certain groups in the state vis-à-vis their access to the ballot. The plaintiffs alleged they were comparatively disenfranchised: in other words, their voting strength as a minority group was diminished or diluted because of the online voting procedure.

Section 2 of the Voting Rights Act prohibits certain groups from imposing standards, practices, or procedures resulting in a denial or abridgement of the right to vote on account of color or race. Through an examination of the facts in the Arizona case, particularly related to the persistence of a digital divide, the plaintiffs argued that Internet voting impairs equal access to the ballot box and has the effect of diluting protected groups' ability to elect candidates of their choice. It should be noted that the Voting Rights

Act protects those groups that have historically faced discrimination in accessing the ballot, outlawing such unsavory practices as the literacy test. The United States Department of Justice has determined that Arizona is a jurisdiction covered by section 5 of the Voting Rights Act, under scrutiny for historic acts of discrimination. New voting procedures, while they may seem innocuous, are under review for their potential discriminatory intent or effect. In this case, the Democratic party's intent in implementing the Internet voting scheme was not challenged. But in its consequence, the voting scheme had the effect of limiting access to the ballot for certain groups, given the disparate access to computers and the Internet across ethnic and racial lines.

The Arizona Democratic party and Election.com succeeded dramatically in increasing overall voter participation. The dot-com spent millions of dollars both on equipment and on outreach, generating excitement in communities whose turnout would otherwise be low. Riding through sparsely populated, poor communities in the equivalent of mobile polling stations outfitted with Internet connections, Election.com representatives mixed marketing sales talk with cheerleading, offering giveaways, and creating a carnival-like atmosphere. A total 86,907 registered Democrats voted in the 2000 primary, compared to 36,072 in 1992 and just 12,844 in 1996. The voter turnout rate in the 2000 primary (10.56 percent) far outpaced the turnout in 1992 (4.30 percent) and 1996 (1.46 percent). In thirty-two of thirty-seven voting districts, turnout was up by at least 5 percent. Election.com reported that 35,768 votes were cast via the Internet. Mail-in ballots numbered 32,159. Fewer than 20 percent of the votes were cast at the polling sites on Saturday, March 11. Of those votes, 13,869 came via traditional paper ballots and 4,174 via the available Internet terminals. The total, based on the 98 percent return figures provided by Election.com, means that 46,028 voters used traditional methods compared to 39,942 who used the Internet.

At first glance, the Arizona experiment would seem like a success. "March 11, 2000, will go down in the history books as a new milestone in the democratic process," said Joe Mohen, chief executive officer of Election.com. "Our goal all along has been to reinvigorate democracy by increasing voter participation and access. We're thrilled that Arizona Democrats showed such a tremendous response to this effort."[13] As impressive as they are, the statistics that have come out of the Arizona vote leave unanswered questions. Is greater turnout using more efficient means a good thing? If we look closely at Arizona, particularly the divide that separates Internet users from the remainder of society, it becomes apparent that not all groups had equal access to Internet voting. Arizona is a state with a large population of Native Americans, many of whom lack basic amenities, such as hot and cold running water and telephone service. The state also has a significant immigrant Hispanic community, many of whom, albeit naturalized, tend to be poorer than the average Arizonan and have scant familiarity with the Internet.

If we look in particular at Internet access across various ethnic and racial groups, it is clear that adult Arizonans did not have an equal opportunity to participate in remote Internet voting. Examining the most recent publicly available data, from the U.S. Census Bureau's December 1998 Current Population Survey as well as from the Arizona Delegate Selection & Affirmative Action Plan of the Arizona Democratic party, it is clear that there are gross inequalities in access to the political process via the Internet.

Non-Hispanic white adults in Arizona are overrepresented on the Internet relative to their population, whereas Hispanics and Native Americans are dramatically underrepresented. Non-Hispanic whites make up 69 percent of the Arizona population but represent 85 percent of adult Internet users in the state; Hispanics make up 21 percent of the state's population but only 10 percent of home Internet users there; and Native Americans represent 6 percent of the population but only 1 percent of Arizona's Internet users.

These facts reveal that while the goal of Internet voting might be legitimate (if outstanding security and authentication issues can be resolved), as currently distributed in the state of Arizona, Internet access leads to unequal opportunity to participate in the political process via the Internet. Three times as many non-Hispanic white adult Arizonans (31 percent) use the Internet from home as Hispanics and Native Americans, a reality that calls into question the practice of Internet voting at this time and place.

Although overall voter participation increased in the state, it is not possible to determine whether the minority vote was diluted in the state because of Internet voting. Unfortunately, the data needed to answer this question are unavailable. What we do know is that the use of the Internet is not open to participation by those without remote Internet access, a disproportionate number of whom are Native American and Hispanic. This unequal access to the Internet by itself has the effect of diluting these minority groups' votes. Of course, overall voter participation would increase if a primary or general election were opened up from one day to multiple days. Since voters only had one day to register their preferences in 1992 and 1996, the increase in turnout in 2000 was probably due in part to the protracted election interval, not just to the use of remote Internet voting.

Many people argue that the Arizona Democratic party was ahead of its time in partnering with Election.com to provide remote Internet voting to galvanize interest in the political process in the state. Certainly, the use of the Internet at this time and in the state of Arizona was novel, but does it advance democratic goals? If Internet voting allows those who are already the most likely to vote, contribute to campaigns, and contact elected officials to amplify their voices, then perhaps Arizona's Democratic party acted prematurely in taking this on. Perhaps a precondition for Internet voting in any geographic region is the assurance of roughly equal access to these communications tools. In particular, those groups that have historically faced discrimination and hardship in getting their voices heard must have reasonable access to the primary mechanisms of participation in the political process.

Twenty years ago, experiments were under way to use the telephone as a way to vote remotely. Certainly, more households in Arizona have telephones than computers with Internet access. So what precipitates the thrust toward Internet voting? One answer lies in the desire of Internet voting companies to brand their products and services in this uncharted (yet potentially lucrative) world. Citizens should be wary in headlong acceptance of this new mode of participation without addressing the persistent unavailability of these tools, and the skills to use them effectively, in our poorest and remotest communities.

The conflict between the desire to use emerging communications tools appropriately to improve the voting process and the rights of individuals to have their political liberties protected brings into relief a central policy challenge of this decade: avoiding the abridgment of people's basic liberties by ensuring that these tools are made ubiquitous and digital literacy skills become commonplace. A Digital Nation must be realized sooner rather than later lest entire communities become marginal to political, economic, and social life.

Often the digital divide has been viewed as just another consumer choice, a gap in consumer buying patterns that will close over time. Yet when these tools are used as vehicles for expressing people's core political rights, or in dispensing critical government services, then these become essential tools, not just another commodity. When the president signed the E-Government Act of 2002,[14] for example, the issues of technology inequality and digital literacy became relevant only as legislators realized that if they wanted to change the relationship between government and citizens, then citizens had to be prepared to engage with their government on electronic terms.

Would any newfangled approach to voting or government service delivery amount to digital disenfranchisement? Many readers might balk at the idea that Internet voting is discriminatory. On the face of it, it opens up another pathway to participation, one that is more convenient than traditional voting. But an aggregate gain needs to be scrutinized in terms of whether there are losers behind the veneer of progress. Are there comparative gains for some groups over others, so that the overall impact of certain groups is weakened because others have more opportunities to participate? So, when government officials seek to contain costs by delivering services electronically, who might lose in the transition from atoms to bits?

In making his decision in the Arizona case, the district judge, Paul G. Rosenblatt, did not dispute the reality of a digital divide in his state. What he had trouble corroborating was whether this digital divide would actually manifest itself in unequal access to the vote. While he agreed that data from the election might reveal that online voting was unfair, the existence of a divide was not sufficient justification, in his opinion, to grant a preliminary injunction. The cautionary note from Judge Rosenblatt should deter future online ventures from rushing headlong into adopting this procedure without addressing the fissures in today's society. In chapter 5, I shed light on certain policies that might shift us closer to the realization of a true Digital Nation so that future elections can benefit from the Internet's democratic potential rather than the Internet's becoming another gatekeeper, like broadcast television, to whom aspiring politicians must pay homage. With a commitment to bold policy initiatives, we can avoid this issue's becoming the new frontier of civil rights work in the twenty-first century.

As Walt Whitman wrote in "Song of Myself," "I speak the pass-word primeval, I give the sign of democracy/By God! I will accept nothing which all cannot have their counterpart of on the same terms." The day will likely come when Internet voting is available on terms acceptable to all. That day has not yet arrived.

E-Government: Build It and They Will Come

In a part of Alabama where joblessness is high, the state employment agency put up billboards to encourage out-of-work people to use a "regional virtual one-stop" center that offered training, job listings, and other assistance.[15] Erected in the poorest region of the state, these advertisements surprised community leaders because the only contact information provided was a Web site address. In a region where many adults are functionally illiterate and without access to the Internet, it was worrisome to residents to see state government offering services in a way that precluded many potential recipients from using them.

Similar situations are revealing themselves at an accelerated rate as more governments experiment with online service delivery. The Secretary of the U.S. Department of Agriculture, Ann Veneman, unveiled a new tool in the arsenal to fight hunger in mid-2003, an online prescreening tool to determine Food Stamp eligibility. The tool takes the respondent through a battery of questions to determine quickly eligibility for nutrition assistance. The irony is that most Food Stamp recipients are not online, and intermediaries who help potential recipients still need to call their local Food Stamp office because the test merely filters out ineligible recipients but does not determine eligibility with certitude. These online tools hopefully are only complements to rather than substitutes for the human touch.

Almost one-quarter of state and federal e-government Web sites nationally offer services that are fully executable online, such as filing taxes, applying for jobs, and renewing driver's licenses.[16] Leading-edge public services include the provision of vital information, health service delivery, and virtual opportunities to learn skills as well as earn credentials and degrees. As the trend away from face-to-face and paper transactions toward electronic service delivery continues, residents without access to electronic platforms (e.g., broadband services and the Internet) or the requisite competencies to use them effectively will be further isolated from the vital services that are pivotal for improving their lives. Currently about 112 million Americans are not online, 90 million are defined as low-literate, 53 million have some level of disability, and 25 million adult residents do not speak English at home. When online government portals present materials at a twelfth-grade level or above without being disability-accessible, and exclusively in English, millions of residents are marginalized from benefits they are constitutionally guaranteed.

The unintended and corrosive consequence is that institutions dedicated to promoting the public good are unwittingly creating the very inequalities they are constitutionally beholden to vanquish. For example, some states have privatized the shift of cash assistance to electronic transfers, a change mandated by Congress in 1996. The result is that some ATMs and grocery stores tack hefty surcharges onto electronic transactions from indigent consumers, many of whom are unbanked and unfamiliar with the use of magnetic strip cards. The tax moratorium on goods purchased online, moreover, is also regressive in penalizing the poor, who must carry the local tax burden.

This important issue needs to be elevated in public discussions and government decision making because it is clear that it is advantageous to all to ensure that e-government initiatives provide opportunities for everyone. In this time of budget shortfalls, if governments save money by transacting business with citizens electronically rather than manually, then clearly it is in their interest to design and promote services that reach deeper into communities. Currently only about 6 percent of state and federal government Web sites offer foreign language translation features; and slightly over one-quarter of Web sites have some form of disability access, which probably means that e-government programs are inadequately serving millions of Americans. There is much to be done, both on the supply and the demand side. On the supply side, technologies need to be made more accessible and ubiquitous, with friendly interfaces and content that is usable to people with disabilities, those who may speak a language other than English, or those who may read at below a fourth-grade level. On the demand side, building skills and developing relevant content are critical. Governments and citizens both win when solutions are devised that are innovative and inclusive, serving the diverse needs, voices, and abilities that characterize the United States of the twenty-first century.

The full force of the law ought to be brought to bear to achieve a Digital Nation. This means discriminatory practices, such as the transfer of government information and services exclusively to cyberspace before all residents can avail themselves of them, ought to be resisted. The new frontier of civil rights is a continuation of old battles, and the technologies ought to be used, where feasible, to organize the resistance against those who for efficiency's sake would foreclose digital opportunity for millions of people.

5

A Digital Nation in Black and White

If we were to view the world in black and white, two contrasting trends would vie to define a fledgling Digital Nation: the forces of consolidation and control, and the manifestation of varied activities favorable to decentralized authority and expression. These tendencies accelerate as economic, political, technological, and social forces collide, accentuating tensions built into the fabric of a commercial republic. After the massive economic expansion of the 1990s, one would have hoped to survey a parallel deepening of democratic vitality. Yet the edifices of consolidation cast longer shadows from which discrete nodes and networks of creativity and expression find it increasingly difficult to escape.

Individuals appear to have greater choice in shaping their own lives—as traditional media like a transistor radio or a black-and-white television become obsolete—yet powerful, often imperceptible chains constrain individuals and communities from determining their own futures. As technology affords people the opportunity to become their own stockbrokers, doctors, or lawyers—making financial, medical, or legal decisions while ensconced in their own entertainment-driven, surround-sound worlds—this newfound freedom plays out before the backdrop of a titanic power struggle for political and economic gain. People are surfing the Web to determine their own wellness prescriptions, for example, while health professionals are hamstrung by behemoth health maintenance organizations that regulate health choices while maneuvering to block any political attempt to expand health coverage to 42 million uninsured Americans.

Examples are legion of this tension; yet the mass media, supposed sentinels of democratic ways of life, are implicated in the process of consolidation in which media owners beholden to powerful financial interests have the power to cover their own misdeeds. After all, they are businesses, participants in a political economy run amok. Many do their civic work only if it increases readership. Who will guard the guardians when they largely control the means of communication and are thus emboldened to muzzle dissent and diversity? A possible answer: the citizen-producer, savvy in the ways of information and communications technologies, marshaling them to organize, energize, and engage sympathizers in diverse causes, often across geographic and class boundaries. The citizen-producer marshals whatever media and technological outlets remain untrammeled and voices perspectives unheard and unseen in the mass media. A Digital Nation policy agenda calls for a democratic and inclusive media and communications culture, one in which alternative perspectives potentially can become conventional. Invigorated by the citizen-producer, a Digital Nation becomes the milieu in which a healthy media and communications culture can be cultivated.

Devolving authority to the citizen-producer should be the hallmark of a Digital Nation agenda. Examining national media and communications policy reveals some accommodation to this mandate: a national information infrastructure is under construction to expand accessibility; demonstration projects exist to jumpstart technology experimentation; and education and training delivering twenty-first-century skills have multiplied. Now at a crossroads, national policymaking also supports increased consolidation of media outlets and information sources, relegating decision making to centralized institutions and geographic regions. Coagulation in the flow of economic, technological, and informational goods bodes ill for the health of democratic culture.

From Black and White to Technicolor

During the period 1993–2001, the national commitment to shaping an inclusive Digital Nation expanded dramatically as information technologies grew in importance as engines of national prosperity.[1] Innovation in information and communications technologies in the 1990s represented a quantum leap in capability, dwarfing in impact the transition from black-and-white to color television. A White House press release of February 2000 declared that "President Clinton believes that we must make access to computers and the Internet as universal as the telephone is today—in our schools, libraries, communities, and homes."[2] In his last year in office,

President Clinton embarked on a tour of impoverished communities, what he called the New Markets Tour, not just to make announcements and sell his domestic information society agenda. Embedded in his approach was a compelling articulation, aimed at industry, of how many poor communities are untapped markets, poised to embrace new products and services, if the appropriate confluence of incentives, support, and community engagement are present. In order to deliver on this promise, the Clinton administration asked Congress for dramatic increases in federal funding to empower communities with digital tools, training, and relevant community content.

Federal funding soared exponentially in the mid- to late 1990s, from tens of millions of dollars to several billions of dollars in fiscal year 2001 (see figure 5.1). During this period, dedicated federal funding for educational technology in the Elementary and Secondary Education Act (ESEA), Title III, increased from $23 million to $872 million.[3] The E-rate program also emerged, plowing nearly $2.25 billion in telecommunications hardware into schools and libraries in poor and rural communities in 2001 alone to connect students and teachers to the Internet.[4] In 1994 the Technology Opportunities Program (TOP) came out of the U.S. Department of Commerce, providing competitive grants totaling $42.5 million in fiscal

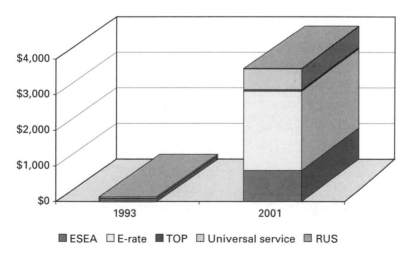

Figure 5.1
Federal Digital Nation Investments, 1993 and 2001 ($ millions)
Source: U.S. Department of Education (2001).

year 2001 to projects demonstrating practical applications of new tele-communications and information technologies serving the public interest. Universal service support mechanisms to assist eligible low-income con-sumers in establishing and maintaining telephone service reached $584 million in 2001.[5] And the U.S. Department of Agriculture's Rural Utilities Service (RUS) launched a grant program providing $15 million for rural distance learning and telemedicine applications as well as local dial-up In-ternet service.[6] As his second term was winding down, President Clinton also outlined a grant program to expand home ownership of networked computers through innovative local public and private partnerships. While this program failed to garner sufficient support, bills continue to propose financing strategies to deepen home ownership of essential communica-tions and computing devices.

Meanwhile, buoyed by the strong economy of the late 1990s, local and state governments invested heavily in civic networks, statewide infrastruc-tures, and educational technology in schools. State ed-tech funding grew steadily until 2003, when aggregate state funding backslid for the first time. Notwithstanding formidable fiscal challenges, some states with pro-gressive leadership continue to invest in communications and computing. Maine, for example, has provided every seventh- and eighth-grade student and teacher with a laptop. Early evidence shows the Maine Learning Tech-nology Initiative "is having many positive impacts on teachers and their in-struction, and on students' engagement and learning."[7] The philanthropic sector, including corporate America, responded to the education and tech-nology gaps left in the wake of the New Economy's breakneck development by taking concrete steps to build a Digital Nation. Supporting everything from high-tech skill building in high schools (Cisco) to community tech-nology centers (AOL Time Warner) to teacher training (Intel), high-tech companies and private foundations invested in schools, community cen-ters, and libraries with hardware, software, permanent staff, and volun-teers to address burgeoning gaps in infrastructure and digital literacy.

In October 1997 the Bill and Melinda Gates Foundation made its first grant in what would become a $200 million effort to outfit library systems in all fifty states, the District of Columbia, and Puerto Rico with hardware and software as well as provide critical technology training, technical assistance, and ongoing support to modernize a flagging library infrastruc-ture. The following year, another major foundation in media and telecommunications, the Markle Foundation, announced its intentions to invest $100 million over three to five years, "a time in which new commercial, cultural, social, and institutional norms will begin to be established for the long term."[8] At the same time, donors such as the MacArthur Foundation and Ford Foundation supported public-interest organizations in Washington, D.C., and elsewhere to promote legislative, legal, and regulatory activity defending public space from its colonization by commercial forces.

These multibillion-dollar public and private initiatives amount to an enormous sunken investment in achieving a Digital Nation, one in which all citizens are empowered to fulfill their life plans. A national information infrastructure now exists, albeit incomplete, networking a critical mass of homes, businesses, schools, libraries, hospitals, governments, and communities. Virtually all schools and libraries are online, and instructional classrooms are far along in offering learners a connection to the outside world.[9] Thousands of community centers offer patrons free access to computer applications and the Internet. A majority of Americans are online, and broadband is reaching more domiciles, serving one in eight Internet-using homes as of 2001, mainly via high-speed cable modems.[10]

Notwithstanding the sheer magnitude of public and private investments in recent years, the problem of unequal access to and effective use of information and technology has not been resolved. Put simply, having tools does not automatically translate into effective and efficient use, as we know from witnessing productivity paradoxes in business and achievement gaps in education where information and communications technologies have been installed. While soaring computer and Internet ownership is a necessary benchmark for success, it does not go far enough in assessing the extent to which individuals have the capacity to achieve fuller participation in an information age economy. One arena where this oversimplification has taken place is in the key indicator measuring progress in educational technology. While connecting K–12 schools to the Internet has been hailed as the key metric of educational technology advancement, this goal tells us little about where the computers are located, how students are using them, the link to academic performance, or teachers' training and pedagogy. Acknowledging the broader context in which problems in unequal information technology access and effective use can be solved can help move us beyond black-and-white solutions and include human-capacity gaps in our policies.

Digital Nation Retrenchment

At this crossroads in the maturation of a democratic Digital Nation agenda, we must evaluate our progress relative to the potential benefits that digital tools can yield. Does sufficient evidence exist to justify continued investment, to leverage the sunken investments of the past to achieve significant productivity and efficiency gains? If so, does the political will exist to make these investments during a time of fiscal austerity and, consequently, the winnowing of domestic policy priorities? We have already covered ground in examining the benefits of widespread digital infrastructure and skill diffusion: the results were positive, if decision makers commit to comprehensive and long-term policies with ample attention paid to equity, human development, and privacy and control issues. However, on political grounds, there is cause for alarm.

After a decade of developing the scaffolding for an inclusive Digital Nation, policymakers began to undermine its foundation in 2001 and 2002. Government and business leaders began to curb funding for infrastructure and training programs. In a relatively short period of time—in the aftermath of the 2000 economic downturn and amidst corporate scandal, the tragedy of September 11, and the subsequent war on terror—the nation was suddenly bereft of leadership on this critical domestic issue. The symbiotic relationship between the dot-com juggernaut and the political momentum to jump-start innovative programs was suddenly broken, with revenue drying up and politicians turning their attention to other domestic and international concerns.

While it would be easy to blame Digital Nation retrenchment on the economic downturn and the war on terror, political considerations were front and center. From the outset, the Bush administration undermined any major initiative identified with its predecessor. Privately, high-ranking officials were hostile to any proposal with a digital divide label, closing the door on any partnership or initiative related to closing the technology gap. In defense of its public position, the Bush administration released an apologia, *A Nation Online,* amounting to an about-face on the Digital Nation agenda. Eager to erase the digital divide language of its predecessor, the U.S. Department of Commerce report eschews any reference to gaps and inequalities in computer and Internet access, focusing instead on the gains made by various subgroups since the previous government technology survey was issued in 2000. The Bush administration touted the fact that a majority of Americans are online as a sign that digital inequality is merely an artifact of early diffusion patterns typical of those of other twentieth-century technology and media.[11] A discussion of continued disparities—and the real impact of these gaps for communities already on the margins of economic and social life—is entirely omitted and thus rejected as a centerpiece of U.S. communications policy.

Buoyed by its invisible-hand approach to e-inclusion, the Bush administration's fiscal budgets proposed reductions in dedicated program funding as the economic downturn and the focus on war siphoned vital resources from the nation's social agenda. Early in the Bush administration's term, large educational technology grant programs were aggregated into block grants to be distributed to the states, with a provision in the legislation giving state decision makers the flexibility to transfer a significant proportion of the funding to other pressing education-related needs. Allowing states flexibility effectively vitiates national technology leadership and reduces real investment considerably.

Another U.S. Department of Education program, the Community Technology Centers (CTC) grant program, was also flung onto the chopping block. Aimed at supporting the burgeoning community technology movement, these grants were designed to seed collaboration and innovation in communities, inviting diverse community organizations to partner in order to provide services more effectively while also addressing sustainability issues. For example, the CTC program at the Mott Community College in Flint, Michigan, partnered with organizations such as the Great Lakes Baptist District Association, the American GI Forum, and the Flint Disability Network to provide basic skills to unemployed residents so they could graduate to the Regional Technology Center to participate in degree programs in electronics, automotive technology, and mechanical engineering. The Disability Network is nationally recognized for its work in helping residents find the right assistive technology to use regular software applications, and its innovative work has generated revenue for the network's technology center in consulting to employers and individuals to match the best assistive technologies to their workforce needs.[12]

Despite the growing body of evidence illustrating the multiplier effects of these community technology alliances—in skill building, service provision, and reaching marginal communities—the Bush administration sought to eliminate the program using the pretext that the program was only marginally effective. This rationale is spurious for two reasons. First, the program had only begun to make grants and have an impact in communities when its cancelation was announced. How can a program be deemed ineffective when it has had scant opportunity to take root? Second, during the time the program's existence was contested in the congressional budget process, the administration changed the program's nature and scope, choosing to focus it on adult education and family literacy. A sleight of hand ensued in which a program originally earmarked to address a broader, more flexible mandate of community empowerment was recast and thus benchmarked against a set of goals not pertinent to its original purpose. Notwithstanding positive evaluations from a highly respected research organization, SRI International, the program continues to be bandied about politically, orphaned by the political establishment.

Attempts to eliminate another Digital Nation program, the Technology Opportunities Program (TOP) in the U.S. Department of Commerce, also highlights the political axe-grinding afoot. While this is another modest program, oscillating between $15 and $45 million during its existence, the Bush administration has questioned its raison d'être. Begun in 1994, TOP has provided matching grants to a wide range of nonprofit organizations—schools, libraries, hospitals, public safety entities, and local and state governments—for projects using technology in innovative ways to solve social problems and improve access to telecommunications tools and networks in underserved communities. The Hays Medical Center in Hays, Kansas, for example, has implemented an in-home telemonitoring system with the goal of reducing posthospital complications and readmissions of recently dismissed, high-risk patients. A project evaluation conducted by Fort Hays State University reveals that readmission rates were lower for the treatment group (e.g., use of the in-home health monitoring system) than for a control group. Total health care costs were also lower for this group.[13] As with the CTC grant program, a prestigious research firm (in this case, the Maryland-based Westat) has conducted ongoing and extensive program evaluations, demonstrating that grantees on the whole met or exceeded their implementation strategies, including meeting the needs of underserved populations not immediately served by the commercial sector.[14] Begun before the Internet was part of the lexicon, TOP promotes an inclusive and innovative information society through demonstrating and shaping the empowering possibilities of communications technologies for marginal communities, which are otherwise ill-prepared to avail themselves of the tools they need to thrive in the information age. Given the infusion of financial and technological resources engendered through broad community collaboration, a TOP grantee may become an anchor tenant in a community. A project connecting schools and parents through a password-protected intranet, for example, may generate household demand for networked computing devices and could sharpen digital literacy skills, a dynamic that may not occur without the spark of community collaboration leading to the infusion of public financial resources.

In a period of rapidly changing technologies, the Bush administration's argument that TOP has fulfilled its mission in demonstrating the usefulness of emerging technologies is peculiar. With technology products becoming faster, more portable, and wireless, the task of showing the social benefits of these tools remains a challenge. With handheld devices, Internet 2, wi-fi and other tools, next-generation venture monies are essential to seed innovation and spur demand to widen the diffusion of digital tools. The use of personal data assistants to monitor homeland security or potential new health pandemics could prevent or mitigate tragedy. But research, development, innovation, and entrepreneurship are all essential to ensure that the next wave of technological advances serves society to the fullest.

Complaints have reverberated that President Bush has not only scuttled the domestic social priorities vis-à-vis a Digital Nation but the industrial policy issues as well. Industry leaders implored the president early in his term to outline a national policy approach to broadband, as the Canadians did in 2001.[15] More generally, the executive branch has failed to frame a national telecommunications and information society agenda similar to the comprehensive, inclusive approach of the Europeans, as outlined in their eEurope pronouncements. Telecommunications decision making has been relegated to the regulatory minutia of federal bureaucrats, with the arbitration of industry disagreements given higher priority than defining and promoting how these technologies of freedom can best serve the public. The National Telecommunications and Information Administration, the executive department responsible for articulating the nation's information society direction, has been eerily silent on an e-inclusion agenda, choosing instead to apply its resources and authority to permit the commercialization of the electromagnetic spectrum. Without benchmarks and goals, it is unclear on what path the nation is headed, short of promoting unbridled deregulation and its most pernicious offspring, consolidation, as the nation has witnessed in the concentration of media power resulting from the repeal of media ownership rules in 1996.[17]

Government retrenchment has proceeded in lockstep with the evisceration of industry's robust social responsibility portfolio, evidenced by the downsizing of corporate foundations that sprang up during the 1990s boom. During the Silicon Valley heyday, active government collaboration in ensuring that the digital revolution would reach everyone meant coaxing and prodding corporate entities to take up their social responsibilities and tap the market potential of underserved communities. U.S. Commerce Secretary William Daley's Digital Divide Conference in December 1999, for example, featured BellSouth Chairman Duane Ackerman and AT&T's Michael Armstrong, both of whom launched major initiatives because their companies were in the national spotlight. Now that the spotlight has been dimmed, companies have jettisoned much of their corporate philanthropy, free from public scrutiny now that attention has been diverted to other domestic priorities.

Many of the corporate vanguards of the late 1990s have shuttered their doors or shrunk substantially. At one time the largest media company in the world, AOL Time Warner, used its market reach and brand recognition to address the information society through strategic grant making as well as innovative nonprofit and consumer-oriented content aimed at meeting social needs. At the time of the AOL/Time Warner merger, Steve Case evoked the image of the Internet as the central feature of the new century's commercial and social life. The Internet, according to Case, would define and shape the twenty-first century, just as Henry Ford and the automobile had done for the twentieth. As part of its philanthropic activities, AOL Time Warner helped spawn the nonprofit PowerUp, an organization dedicated to building the skills and self-esteem of young people by jumpstarting thousands of community technology centers across the United States. Launched in November 1999 amid great fanfare, PowerUp outfitted several thousand centers with telecommunications services, computers, and access to the Internet before closing three years later. Its demise, coupled with steady attacks on the federal Community Technology Centers grant program, pose formidable sustainability challenges to the field of community technology, as centers scramble to raise funds to pay for the recurring costs generated by their own success and the oscillating fortunes of corporate America. In early 2003 the AOL Time Warner Foundation closed its Dulles offices, laid off its staff, and consolidated its activities in a small staff in New York City. Other major corporate foundations have followed a similar course, because of reduced stock value, threatening the sustainability of community and school-based technology efforts.

Not just political and economic considerations but the very nature of charitable giving militates against forging a long-term commitment to a Digital Nation agenda. Philanthropic institutions generally fund initiatives for several years at best and then turn their attention elsewhere, often leaving grantees with daunting financial challenges. Exceptions exist, such as the Bernard van Leer Foundation, which takes a long-term developmental perspective on its grant making, but the norm is for short-term commitments, saddling nonprofits with the burden of finding financing to sustain their efforts. The Markle Foundation's decision to increase the amount of payout over three to five years, for instance, is probably the minimum amount of time necessary to witness appreciable change amid the turbulent political and economic forces at work to commercialize the digital landscape. On the whole, foundations balk at supporting advocacy work to alter the legislative climate or the legal framework, fearful of crossing the IRS, transgressing lobbying restrictions, offending corporate board members, or being tarred in the media. Thus, they often operate on the margins of political change, choosing to fund research rather than advocacy work. Attempts to alter the behavior of corporations by leveraging foundation dollars, such as the Markle Foundation's attempt to influence the design and content of violent and antisocial videogames aimed at youth, are often ineffective. The scope of investment is too small relative to the billions of dollars in revenue companies like Sony earn from product sales. Clearly, there is an urgent need for foundations to sharpen their model of social change, sort out the most effective approaches to improve the media environment, and work collectively to attain tangible outcomes, with modest resources.

Meanwhile, the Bill and Melinda Gates Foundation's U.S. Library Program is being curtailed, challenging libraries to find new ways to modernize their equipment, train their staff, and promote their offerings after the world's richest foundation has exited the scene. The foundation's departure could not have come at a worst time for many library systems as state policymakers struggle to maintain government services amid the worst fiscal crisis in recent memory. Oftentimes in budget crises, infrastructure and training are among the first investments to be slashed, a danger to a Digital Nation because these are its lifeblood. State legislatures' decisions to prune California's Internet 2 project aimed at K–20 education, the Digital California Project, or Wisconsin's Technology for Educational Achievement (TEACH) program means that for all intents and purposes sunken investments will be trimmed so aggressively that they will lose their viability.[18]

In a deflationary economic climate, rosy assumptions regarding the diffusion of technology are discredited. The global economic slowdown has affected technology investment and diffusion dramatically. For the first time since the Internet became familiar to consumers, zero or negative growth in penetration is occurring, particularly in low-income households where consumers are forced to choose among an array of communications services, including mobile, land line, cable, and Internet offerings. As households jettison their land line telephone service to pay for the convenience of mobile telephony, for example, they may also lose their Internet provider in one fell swoop. Unless the price of bundled services drops, low-income consumers will make hard choices to stay connected. According to the Pew Internet & American Life Project,

Internet penetration rates have hovered between 57 percent and 61 percent since October 2001, rather than pursuing the steady climb that they had showed in prior years. One possible explanation for this leveling trend is that the number of people dropping offline roughly equals the number of newcomers who come online each month. The lack of growth might also be tied to a struggling economy that leaves some families worried about household finance. Or it may be that we have reached a point where the adoption curve has peaked and the market is no longer working to bring online new groups of Internet users.[19]

Unlike *A Nation Online,* which forecasts nothing but blue skies vis-à-vis Internet diffusion, the Pew report forces policymakers to take a closer look at the scope and direction of national efforts to achieve a Digital Nation. Clearly, if we are taking two steps forward *and* two steps back, Internet churn rates and the diminishing economic capacity of millions of Americans must be addressed through new public and private strategies to jump-start demand for services. With much of the high-tech and telecommunications sectors in financial turmoil, corporate boards and Wall Street investors frown on the deployment of high-speed networks in hard-to-serve communities, such as Indian Country or the Mississippi Delta.

Demand-side solutions have also largely failed, because corporate marketers have yet to find the killer apps to mobilize consumer appetite for some new telecommunications and media services.

A good deal of the failure of information society policy revolves around the top-down nature of many investments. By definition, marginalized communities tend to be outside the economic, technological, and informational flows typical of activity at the center of society. Thus it is unsurprising that many on the fringe say the Internet is irrelevant to their daily lives. Rather than attracting more communities with diverse service offerings, one-size-fits-all templates or wholesale solutions are put forward, dampening the appetite of untapped markets. A rich dialogue between potential media and technology providers and the community might lead to customized solutions, perhaps tools jointly developed and owned by communities and their media partners.[20] As large commercial providers of broadband services struggle to find the applications and content for which consumers will pay, communities are taking this issue on, grappling with innovative ways to build and maintain their own networks, with content partly percolating from stakeholders in the community. The Commonwealth Broadband Collaborative (CBC) in eastern Massachusetts is partnering with several community-based organizations who are building a public telecommunications network, and training individuals and organizations to produce their own content and meet their collective needs through the media.

Bottom-up, community-driven approaches such as the CBC are slow to catch on because they are labor-intensive and often inimical to the business models of corporate and government officials. Recent debates on low-power radio[21] and spectrum management[22] highlight the tension between for-profit entities bent on parceling the ether as a commodity and public-interest groups who want to carve out open spaces to homestead, build community, and express the widest variety of voices and perspectives through the media. Often this more comprehensive approach comes through the back door as policymakers with grandiose visions of, say, electronic service delivery witness their visions crash head on with the digital divide and skills gaps among prospective beneficiaries of these services. So, with e-government rollout at the local, state, and national levels, many policymakers support headlong the assertion that these mechanisms will shave costs and expand services but fail to see that many of their constituents will be unable or unwilling to avail themselves of these services. When mainstream policymakers are stymied in fulfilling their own mandates—cost-saving technological solutions such as e-health, e-government, and distance education—they are forced to address the impediments to the realization of these goals in U.S. neighborhoods and communities.

Building Bridges and Connecting the Dots

The Telecommunications Act of 1996 is a linchpin of Digital Nation policymaking in the United States, promoting the rollout of basic and advanced services to homes, elementary and secondary schools, libraries, and rural health centers. Universal service disbursements tallied $5.3 billion in 2002. Yet if telecommunications approaches are disconnected from educational, economic, and social policymaking, infrastructure investments will fall short of achieving the potential benefits from integration with core policy arenas. The enabling potential of media and technology, when integrated into functional policy arenas such as education and health delivery, is the "sweet spot" where the power of a Digital Nation will be realized.

If we examine the mandate of the universal service fund for schools and libraries, commonly known as the E-rate, the challenge of coordination and integration will quickly become apparent. First, because the E-rate is a program in which common carriers collect surcharges from consumers—fees later disbursed to eligible educational institutions, among others—the types of services on offer to schools are limited and exclude computing devices, content, and training. While the universal service fund might be a consistent revenue stream, the advantages of a $10 billion educational investment are tempered when educational wares are limited and must be supplemented in substantial proportions to add value to teaching and learning.

Schools can apply for three buckets of services: internal connections, telecommunications services, and Internet connections. Most E-rate funding is designated for internal connections, the acquisition of equipment and services for internal building networks, such as connectors, switches, routers, local-area networks, and servers. Only 10 percent of discounts are allocated to the cost of Internet access, suggesting that schools are in the early stages of developing an infrastructure supportive of good educational technology practice.[23] Second, the structural separation between the Federal Communications Commission, a quasi-independent regulatory body of lawyers and regulators, and the executive branch makes it exceedingly difficult to synchronize agendas. So, executive department budgets and legislative priority setting for social policy tend to show little acquaintance with telecommunications provisions.

What is worse, many policymakers in Washington equate a Digital Nation agenda with an infrastructure development strategy: ensuring that low-cost, high-speed telecommunications services are ubiquitous. In the 108th Congress, the Senate Communications Committee, led by Montana Senator Conrad Burns, set its priorities vis-à-vis digital empowerment: preserving a viable universal service fund for rural America and allowing broadband vendors to expense a percentage of their investments, allowing for immediate deduction of a capital expenditure rather than along a normal depreciation schedule. Many rural Senators embrace broadband diffusion as a critical public good to buttress economic development in far-flung communities. In a weekly newsletter on the topic of the digital divide, for example, Maine Senator Olympia Snowe described the gap between haves and have-nots as basically a broadband divide: "While efforts are being made to ensure broadband services are available in all regions—both urban and rural—the fact is that these services . . . are being deployed more rapidly in urban areas . . . without action by Congress, this discrepancy is likely to become more pronounced."[24] The same week that Snowe, a Republican, issued her remarks, the Congressional Democrats issued their "E-Strategy for Economic Growth" document, which identified as its first goal "to make broadband Internet available to every American by the end of the decade."

Policy programs of national scope and significance thus have focused primarily on installing infrastructure, from narrowband to broadband, with a smattering of funds dedicated to training teachers and to socially beneficial applications. In the arena of K–12 technology expenditure, for example, of the $7.2 billion spent in fiscal year 1998 (approximately 30 percent of which came from the national government), about $51 million went for software and $29 million (about 4 percent) for training expenses and release time for teachers.[25] This figure is sobering when juxtaposed with a recent report suggesting that at least 30 percent of ed-tech budgets be devoted to professional development.[26] Clearly, the basic building blocks facilitating universal access and effective use of information and communications technologies—what former Vice President Al Gore called the Internet ABCs (Access, Basic Training, and Content)—need to be more fully supported. Given the oversupply of hardware relative to the human capital, content, and applications needed to optimize the infrastructure development, substantial investments are needed to harness the network for public purposes. Of the $3.7 billion national investments in 2001, as illustrated in figure 5.1, over 90 percent flows to expanding infrastructure while training and content capture only a trickle of the total funding stream.

With such overinvestment in infrastructure relative to training and content, it is unsurprising that productivity gains and other benefits are often hard to pinpoint. At a recent workshop in Budapest, Hungary, a group of education leaders from various member countries of the Organization for Economic Cooperation and Development (OECD) debated the relationship between information and communications technologies and educational outcomes for underserved youth; most of them lamented the lack of support for longitudinal research, quantitative and ethnographic, to gauge the benefits of technology over time. The prevailing wisdom is not that information and communications technologies and performance are unrelated. Rather, most investments to date have not embedded technology and media sufficiently into education and learning over a long enough period to engender change in student performance.

The surest way to redress the imbalance between hardware and humanware is to leverage the public and private infrastructure investments with training, content development, stronger links with social service deliverers, and organizational capacity building. The recent proliferation of community technology centers, for example, expands the need for well-trained staff to manage these venues and provide technical assistance as machines inevitably break down. According to one report, libraries and community centers are much more likely to be used by lower-income residents and minorities for job-related and educational purposes than their more affluent, nonminority cohorts.[27] These venues are playing an increasingly important role in providing access to technology, employment assistance, skills development, and even social services,[28] raising the stakes for these centers to be fully funded, well staffed, and high-performing institutions.[29]

It is clear from the private-sector perspective that national and state policymakers must step into the breech to help sustain extant programs. If governments retrench, stripping training and technology funding from tight budgets, then private investors may well be discouraged from supporting new initiatives. The infusion of technology into schools through E-rate discounts has resulted in a geometric increase in the demand for professional development.[30] And in libraries, where funds are increasingly difficult to come by, library professionals must have financial support and professional development opportunities to bolster their skills in assisting patrons and to discourage attrition.[31] Clearly, to safeguard such activities, public and private engagement should be embraced and incentivized, where appropriate.

As taxpayers continue to support universal service programs, including the E-rate, the question must be asked, How can we ensure that this nascent telecommunications infrastructure will become a useful tool to serve the educational goals and proven pedagogical techniques of good teachers? Clearly, the E-rate can be leveraged most dramatically, first, if teachers are well trained to use the Internet effectively and to integrate the tools, where appropriate, into curriculum and, second, if schools extend these tools to a broader community to maximize citizens' access. On the first point, professional development, both in-service and preservice training, must be extended and strengthened at the national level. The only national program aimed at innovative preservice technology training for teacher was eliminated in 2002 at a time when these programs became essential. Information technology should be mobilized as a tool in enhancing professional development, for example, through broadband delivery of master teachers' lesson plans to the classrooms of at least the 150,000 new teachers hired annually at U.S. public schools. Regarding the second point, certain school systems are paving the way and using the money saved by the E-rate discount to expand after-school programs open to neighborhood residents. State governments should explore inexpensive and incremental ways to leverage the benefits accruing from national outlays in computer access points through such ventures as funding for staff to supervise after-school instruction and covering liability insurance, as California State Senator Debra Bowen has proposed.[32] Finally, more attention must be paid both to raising awareness and engaging in outreach in communities to spur demand for existing services in community.

Libraries are also receiving E-rate discounts and are leveraging federal, state, and private monies in order to flourish in the information age. While funding has been cut for libraries in some states and localities, other communities have had dramatic success in passing bond measures and other library-support projects. The Library Services and Technology Act (LSTA) provides the best opportunity for libraries to preserve and extend their ability to remain relevant to their communities by strengthening the role technology plays in expanding and enhancing information services. What happens to libraries after one-time grants wane is a critical question in an age of shrinking support for public institutions. With about $200 million invested to date in libraries for technology infrastructure, training, technical assistance, and support, can the Gates Foundation find partners who appreciate its sunken investment and who can help sustain libraries' ascension into the digital age? State funds also need to be parlayed to extend library hours to expand access to information tools, both print and electronic.

In order for the telecommunications network to be optimized, decision makers in industry, governments, and philanthropy must address policy solutions that scale and sustain early successes. Early successes are identified based on rigorous research, evaluation, and assessment, all of which are often undervalued when funding is meager. "Best practices" run the gamut and use various strategies to parlay funding. Many creative community technology centers, for example, forge collaborations that allow them to offer classes to local residents, potentially creating new revenue streams. For example, a center in El Centro, California, trained CalWorks members in computer applications and résumé building, thereby diversifying their funding base. Covering the ongoing operating budget of centers is probably untenable for a single private funder; therefore, public partnerships and revenue generation models should be explored as longer-term solutions to sustainability. Also, with an emphasis on volunteer mentors and staff, community technology underwriters should explore ways to generate wider networks of private-sector volunteers, perhaps by exploring a matchmaker service that would mobilize the standing army of information technology professionals and other volunteers where demand and need is greatest.

As these projects lift off and go to scale, the challenge of sustainability looms. While firming up volunteers and mentors is critical, private-public partnerships must also be forged to pay for staffing, the digitization of content, and cutting-edge applications. Just as Andrew Carnegie's huge investments in libraries was greeted by a public that fell in love with these institutions and was willing to bootstrap his investment, one would hope that the huge outlays being made in formal and informal learning institutions would be leveraged by local, state, and national politicians.

In addition, because of negative externalities in the poorest communities that make private-sector investment unlikely in the short term, the public sector should facilitate new investment, in the form of expanded universal service in hard-to-serve communities as well as public venture funds to spur socially beneficial innovation. The universal service fund, including the E-rate, has yielded dividends in extending basic and advanced telecommunications services to disadvantaged areas of the nation, but these programs must be linked to real-world outcomes, such as economic or educational improvement, and expanded to more informal learning institutions. A technology liaison in the federal government might provide an invaluable service in creating stronger links between diverse, standalone programs, such as closing the gap between educational and telecommunications policy.

Of course, implementing many of these policy steps takes taxpayer support and political will. While the 2001 budget surplus has vanished, survey data reveal that a majority of Americans support the use of public funds to expand public access and training for underserved communities. Fifty-four percent of Americans believe that communities should provide more places where the public can access the Internet; fully two-thirds of adults support the use of tax dollars to fund Internet access in libraries; and three-quarters of adults support the use of tax dollars to train teachers to use new technology. Research on the public's commitment to libraries also reveals that a plurality of Americans favor spending extra tax dollars for library services, such as computer access and information.[33]

Will national policymakers step up to the challenge? Bills continue to be floated in Congress to expand digital opportunity, proposing everything from using public properties, such as the U.S. Postal Service, to provide kiosks to expand access to government information, to tax credits for low- and middle-income households who purchase computers. An enduring challenge is to summon the funds to support large-scale initiatives. Some visionaries propose to use the proceeds from the auction of the publicly owned spectrum to fund programs, existing and prospective, to empower a Digital Nation agenda. The resale of the analog spectrum as broadcasters' mandatory transition to digital looms could yield tens of billions of dollars for public-interest purposes, and the auctioning of advanced commercial mobile services would fully fund Digital Nation initiatives for years to come. But realizing such an ambitious goal will depend strongly on federal leadership and long-term vision, qualities that seem to be waning at a time when they are most in demand.

6

Flattening the Virtual Landscape in Education

In educational settings worldwide, information and communications technologies are playing an expanding role—from mundane back end procurement to the extraordinary possibilities of the virtual school. Weaving these tools into educational practice remains a relatively young enterprise, its potential largely untapped in renewing teaching and learning.[1] Technologists forecast an emerging world of pervasive, portable networked computing, customized tools, and intelligent machines that will soon make the desktop computer appear antiquated. While these tools promise breakthroughs in the manner and degree to which lifelong learning occurs, concerted action is required among governments, civil society organizations, and private enterprise to bring about a Digital Nation, to ensure that new tools and devices do not exacerbate divides in learning opportunities and outcomes within and between communities and countries.

Most if not all of the industrialized countries in the Organization for Economic Cooperation and Development (OECD) face daunting challenges at the dawn of the new century to cultivate learning societies meeting the acute needs of disadvantaged populations. Young people with learning disabilities, immigrants, the indigent, victims of war and civil unrest, the disaffected, and the incarcerated can all benefit from expanding access to and effective use of information and communications technologies. Groups pushed out of formal schooling owing to social stigma, such as pregnancy or bullying, have found more supportive settings for learning in cyberspace, such as the successful Not-School.net project in the United Kingdom.[2] Incarcerated youths and those under court supervision in the United States are telling their stories with digital cameras and multimedia, building self-esteem and restoring their social footing in an environment in which many feel marginalized and disposable.[3] And significant rates of youth depression and disaffection in the former Soviet Union and Eastern Europe have led to promising experiments with individualized interactive software to approach, analyze, and treat social anxiety in a safe environment.[4]

In each of these experiments, outcomes have improved dramatically for youths who, for whatever reason, languished in formal schooling. Importantly, from a policy perspective, entrepreneurial leadership promoting alternative approaches to learning have demonstrated success, thus meriting recurring support from governmental and other large funding sources. In this respect, alternative approaches are becoming mainstream because of persuasive change agents' breaking through with support from public and private underwriters. These programs—creative after-school programs, break-the-mold new learning institutions, and the like—have pressured monolithic school systems to change, with demands for quality and innovation coming from parents, students, and concerned citizens who have been energized by what they have seen. The Intel-supported Computer Clubhouse network, for example, has established modestly successful, creative after-school programs where disadvantaged teenagers work with mentors to design and create robotics, art, music, and video using technology in collaborative, supportive environments.[5] Given that these experiences are often foreign to school day learning rituals, stakeholders are beginning to build bridges—pedagogical, technological, and social—between school day and after-school programs.

Formidable obstacles must be overcome to take to scale some of these promising programs, not the least of which is the pervasive discrimination and marginalization facing many subgroups in society. More broadly, youth stereotypes require revision with an eye toward treating youths as critical assets and responsible partners in building the learning society.[6] Many of these corrosive frames of reference (e.g., the frequent mass media depiction of youths as delinquents, not future assets) impinge on the allocation of resources directed at the edification of hard-to-serve young people. In this climate, raising performance levels and softening the impact of economic disadvantage and social stigma will require us to see youths in a new light and to allocate resources accordingly. Programs such as the Intel Computer Clubhouse network and Not-School.net honor youths as future assets with huge untapped potential, to be unlocked in part through self-directed, project-based learning.

The Challenges of Raising Performance

In many instances, new computing devices and communications networks are introduced into educational systems unprepared to integrate them effectively to improve performance, particularly for low-achieving learners. Outworn organizational structures and human-capacity deficits often prevent forward progress in learning. Poor teacher morale and qualifications coupled with shortages of material and educational resources also hinder the effective integration of technology and ultimately hold back student performance.[7] Low-achieving students with limited exposure to computing devices are clearly less likely to benefit from them than students with greater time on task. The quality of physical infrastructure, finally, including electrical upgrades and building maintenance, affects technology diffusion.[8] Parachuting information and communications technologies into these environments without addressing underlying issues of organizational readiness, continuous professional development, and infrastructure would be precipitous. A significant period of time is required to integrate ed-tech across academic subjects—allowing for the development of technology plans, management training, and professional development—a painstaking process requiring patience on the part of decision makers as these changes come to bear on institutional cultures.

More often than not, teachers feel unready to integrate computer networks into the classroom.[9] Few opportunities exist for continuous learning for many time-crunched teachers. In high-poverty school districts in the United States, many teachers lack the pedagogical, academic, and class management skills to instruct low-achieving students. And widespread teacher shortages, where demand outstrips the supply of new teachers from training schools, thwart the imperative to raise the quality of the teaching cohort. In initial teacher training, moreover, ed-tech instruction is patchy, at least in Europe[10] and the United States.

It is not uncommon for pupils to express frustration because they can outperform their instructors with the tools.[11] Rather than serving as a source of tension, young people's fluency with technology should be channeled into creative mentoring programs where youths can tutor their peers and seniors alike, such as the successful Senioren @ns Netz program in Leipzig or a promising experiment in Bonn called Computer Training for Underserved Youths.[12] In after-school and community-based programs, which draw many disillusioned and under-performing youths, organizational readiness and staff training are quite uneven (as are public and private budget commitments), with clear implications for introducing new learning tools into educational and social work aimed at disadvantaged youths. Organizations such as the Education Development Center's YouthLearn Initiative in the United States and the Digital Chances Foundation in Germany have developed manuals and courses for youth center staff, the latter also running a telephone hotline to provide technical assistance where appropriate.[13]

While the challenges of professional development are daunting, examples of successful practice do exist. Beginning in 1997 the state of Idaho required 90 percent of all certified personnel in a school to pass one of three state-approved technology assessment models by 2001. Through robust collaboration with state colleges of education in the preparation and in-service training of teachers as well as creative integration of technology into instructional practices, this goal has been achieved. With 15,000 teachers in geographically dispersed districts in the state and only twenty training staff in the colleges, creative distance programs and train-the-trainer models proved successful in meeting the state government's proficiency goals for teachers.[14] In Finland, according to Jouni Kangasniemi at the Finnish Ministry of Education, approximately 20 percent of teachers receive government-funded advanced in-service training every year, a €2.5 million program complementing institutionally supported professional development.

In most networked-ready economies (as the World Economic Forum calls economies poised to reap dividends in productivity resulting from information technologies),[15] substantial investments in infrastructure preceded any serious initiative to train teachers effectively in their use. The goal to wire every classroom was ensconced in national policymaking in the United States beginning in 1994 with the launch of a variety of public and private initiatives. Training and curriculum development have hitherto played catch up. In the United States[16] and virtually every European country except Finland,[17] federal infrastructure expenditures greatly outpace investments in human-capacity building. In short, technology investments often trump training the cadre of teachers who will effectively integrate these tools.

In this milieu, the theme of technology and equity is of critical importance to policymakers and other decision makers because technology can provide a platform to equalize access to resources and opportunities to learn, leading to a true Digital Nation. Article 26 of the Universal Declaration of Human Rights states that everyone has a right to an education directed to the full development of the human personality.[18] In order to ensure equal educational opportunity, adequate facilities and resources, technological and otherwise, are required, as well as a shared belief in equal dignity and respect for the inherent ability of all peoples to learn. In the U.S. context, recent debates over school equity have proceeded along two fronts: the "resource parity" argument suggests that per-pupil expenditures ought to be roughly equal and flow from a fair tax or revenue model; and the educational "adequacy" approach looks at resource inputs (e.g., teacher pay, class size, facilities) and student performance outcomes as bellwethers for courts to determine whether school systems are inadequate and thus unconstitutional.[19]

Indicative of the raison d'être for the civil rights and equity movements are wide achievement gaps in many OECD countries, differentials particularly acute in Germany and the United States, for example, where substantial variation in reading achievement exists between the highest one-quarter of students and the lowest.[20] Student performance is strongly correlated with economic, social, and cultural status[21] as are access to and frequent use of computers and the Internet.[22] One might expect in the short term, therefore, that these technologies would contribute to a widening, not a shrinking, of the achievement gap unless successful programs are ramped up to provide motivation and technical fluency while simultaneously offering remediation in cognitive skills development and core academic subjects. Without comprehensive and systemic policy strategies for e-learning, it remains to be seen at the macro level how strategic investments in information networks may mitigate these gaps. Clearly, targeted interventions are necessary to address at-risk young people's complex emotional, social, and academic needs (including in-school and out-of-school young people, the latter largely underskilled and underemployed), and information and communications technologies can play a vital role in facilitating these interventions.[23] Yet some policy leaders are increasingly normalizing instructional approaches and assessments[24] at this critical juncture in which ed-tech has begun to exhibit promise in customizing solutions to learners' diverse cognitive and environmental profiles.[25]

The good news is that many young people across the board are attracted to technology: it sparks their curiosity in learning and may even provide a turning point—that is, a healthy discontinuity in the experience of social disadvantage—as Professor Alexander Grob of the University of Bern has argued.[26] At the micro level, innovation has yielded transformational results for many underserved youths, with the promise of closing the achievement gap for learners served by good programs.[27] Technology has been instrumental in expanding self-esteem and feelings of self-efficacy.[28] Successful practice, where leadership interventions break the cycle of poor performance and underachievement using computing devices, are, however, exceptional, reaching only a small portion of the millions of disadvantaged youths and young adults in OECD countries. Where inspired leadership has met with success is in programs that take a concentrated, systemic approach, empowering staff and students to co-conspire in school renewal. Given that information and communications technologies are capital-intensive investments, these reforms require dedicated funds (a combination of reallocated and new revenues) through a mix of constant public and private sources.

One example from the United States of a school district undergoing marked transformation because of creative uses of ed-tech and communications tools is the Union City School District in New Jersey, across the river from New York City. Robust collaborations from a variety of partners, including deep community partnerships, as well as a strong steering role for staff, led to the decision over several years of planning to implement comprehensive curriculum reform, major scheduling changes, increased in-service training, and an infusion of technology into homes as well as schools to enhance cooperative learning.[29] A school district that in 1989 did less well than the state average with respect to attendance, dropout and transfer rates, and standardized test scores was transformed: today its eighth-grade readiness test results are among the highest in the state. This is a harbinger of a Digital Nation in which technology invites the metamorphosis of outworn institutions.

The level of technology infusion occurring in Union City could not have happened without dedicated resources. As Fred Carrigg, executive director for the district's academic programs, declared, "None of this happens without money, but a lot of that can be and should be a restructuring of how money is expended."[30] First, in 1989 the state courts found the funding and resource levels for schools in poor communities to be inadequate and hence unconstitutional. The subsequent increase in per-pupil expenditure allowed Union City to experiment with new approaches to learning, including implementing comprehensive curriculum reform focusing on a literacy curriculum to sharpen thinking, reasoning, and collaboration skills. Second, other state and federal funding for high-poverty communities was leveraged. And finally, Bell Atlantic (now Verizon, the largest telecommunications company in the United States) made substantial hardware investments in schools and homes in order to explore how pervasive technology diffusion would affect learning.

One lesson to draw from the U.S. experience in general and from Union City in particular is that successful policy approaches need to be comprehensive and holistic: they must empower stakeholders and address youth development in its broadest sense. Union City leadership turned the established order on its head—in deputizing staff to make decisions at the school level; in altering the cadence of the school day; in building bridges to the home and broader community—so that students from the toughest backgrounds could excel in this new environment. In the United States and Germany, the desire to develop more comprehensive and scalable learning experiences has resulted in extending the school day to allow youths and the community to access facilities, including networked computers, in the after-school environment. The 21st Century Community Learning Centers program in the United States and a new initiative in Germany to extend school hours in the afternoon both address the challenge of enhancing student achievement while also searching for more inclusive approaches to bridge the world of formal and community-based learning.

Comprehensive and sustainable approaches have proven elusive because of some combination of the following inauspicious circumstances: turnover in leadership; uncertainties in budgets and prioritization; and fragmentation of programs and policies, leading to unevenness in the maturation and effectiveness of programs across the board.

Cross-Country Comparisons: Finland, Germany, and the United States

Can information and communications technologies be drivers to close achievement gaps and address the range of needs of underserved youths as a matter of effective national policymaking? Or is this fated to be a piecemeal exercise, dependent on the exigencies of local circumstances, washed along by the current of inexorable social forces? I explore national policymaking in three OECD countries, Finland, Germany and the United States, for signs that information and communications technologies can be an important component in strategic interventions in the downward spiral of social exclusion afflicting too many young people. Germany and the United States suffer from significant social divides, the former in part because of reunification effects, the latter in part because of historical discrimination against racial and ethnic minorities. Do we witness signs that computer networks are mitigating these gaps? Finland is juxtaposed with Germany and the United States as a country with a relatively modest variation in performance across a range of economic, social, and cultural variables. Have new technologies played a role in achieving this egalitarian state of affairs?

In cities in the United States and Germany, demographic shifts in urban centers, coupled with job flight to the suburbs and the loss of manufacturing jobs due to automation and business migration, signal tumultuous times for low-skilled urban youths.[31] Successful strategies to mitigate these inequalities focus on macro-level fiscal policies, such as tax policies, broadening educational and workforce preparation opportunities (where an adequate tax base and public support for education exist), and cultivating an attractive business climate for entrepreneurs and innovators to blossom.[32] In short, promising government policy embarks on initiatives to raise performance while softening the impact of socioeconomic disadvantage. One favorable lesson from Germany, given its low youth unemployment rate relative to other OECD countries, is to get youths into jobs early and to keep them employed.[33]

Germany and the United States possess significant achievement gaps, and it is worth examining whether effective use of computing devices and communications networks is mitigating these differences and effectively equalizing educational opportunities and outcomes. One can adduce striking examples of effective practices: Union City or the Web.Punkte project in Bremen, Germany, is a good example. At the macro level, various support programs such as the E-rate in the United States and Germany's New Media in Education program aim to stimulate ed-tech access and effective use in schools. Various clusters of private-sector investments, such as Intel's Computer Clubhouse program in the United States, have proved crucial. In Germany, Deutsche Telekom and the Federal Ministry of Education and Research initiated a public-private venture in 1995 called Schulen ans Netz, offering 10,000 schools free Internet access (for one year) and one multimedia PC. So many programs exist, but what difference have they made?

Strategies to harness the potential of technology for educational advancement in OECD countries began in earnest in the mid-1990s. The Clinton administration ushered in the National Information Infrastructure (NII), promising to connect institutions and streamline service delivery. Between 1993 and 2001 national funding in the area of educational technology and universal service soared from $23 million to over $3.5 billion,[34] almost all of which was aimed at economically, socially, and culturally marginalized communities. Categorical funding has since declined,[35] as has state funding,[36] yet overall federal education funding has increased significantly, including more funding for teacher training.[37] Other countries entered the fray at roughly the same time. In Finland the first national information society strategy document was written with the backdrop of the recession of 1993–94. At this time in Germany, Chancellor Kohl was focusing more on digital television than on computerization.[38] Four years later, in 1998, Chancellor Schröder, in his first statement as head of government, underscored the central importance of spreading the fruits of the information society to all residents. The prevailing educational technology doctrine came to be premised on accomplishing three interrelated goals, what Vice President Gore called the Internet ABCs: achieving universal *access* to information and communications tools; expanding *basic training* for teachers; and ensuring that relevant *content* would be produced to optimize network use. Similarly, the German model was predicated on three pillars to support the modern school: infrastructure, competence, and content.[39]

In implementing this three-pronged approach, it remained unclear what an appropriate balance among the three would resemble in terms of funding and sequence, particularly to diffuse knowledge and skills, not just technology. In the United States this question was answered de facto by the passage of the Telecommunications Act of 1996, in which the E-rate provided significant resources for telecommunications infrastructure diffusion. The program's purpose is to expand universal service and essential communications tools to schools and libraries according to economic need and geographic isolation. Operating on a sliding scale, with recipients (e.g., state education agencies, school districts, individual schools, and library systems) eligible for a discount of up to 90 percent on certain telecommunications services, including telephony and Internet service, E-rate discounts vary depending on the degree of poverty and rurality.[40] Eligible educational institutions apply for the discounts or reimbursements from a nongovernmental organization set up to administer the fund.

The priority for much of this funding was in meeting the goal of modernizing infrastructure in schools, a goal now accomplished in a quantitative sense for both schools and libraries in the United States, the latter due in large measure to the work of the Bill and Melinda Gates Foundation. With such a large investment targeting infrastructure development, school systems quickly scrambled to train teachers and develop curriculum, tasks falling by and large to local, regional, and state educational agencies.

School systems with the expertise, economies of scale, or flexibility to develop technology plans tied to curricular and school reform goals were often able to garner enough public and private support to begin to implement programs to affect student performance markedly. As was clear from the Union City example, ubiquitous communications tools linking the school to the larger community, including the household, expanded learning— and the accountability for learning—to the larger community, greatly increasing parent and caregiver involvement in the educational enterprise.

In September 1999, Germany released its comprehensive strategy for the information society, a master plan called "Innovation and Jobs in the Information Society of the 21st Century."[41] The program defines specific targets through 2005, including increasing Internet subscribership, equipping schools with multimedia PCs, developing a leading position worldwide in education software development, and integrating the new media into a renewed approach to lifelong learning.[42] Installing hardware was a priority, propelled by partnerships with industry (e.g., Deutsche Telekom provided ISDN and some DSL connections to schools), including the creation of a marketplace for new and second-hand PCs.

Popularized and promoted by Chancellor Schröder in 2000, the Internet for All [Internet für Alle] ten-point campaign aimed to articulate the benefits of computers and the Internet through public education campaigns, thereby countering the dangers inherent in unwittingly fostering digital inequality by targeting specific underserved groups: senior citizens, people with disabilities, immigrants, women, and the indigent. A national outreach program, however, is tempered by the fact that schools and other learning institutions are run by local governments, churches, and nonprofit organizations. For the most part, funds are not provided to link local activities to the national campaign, let alone to sustain their efforts.

What the Internet for All campaign found was that Internet "objectors" constitute almost half of the German population over 14 years old. This category of objectors is heterogeneous, comprising diverse demographic groups with differing rationales for not using the Internet.[43] A large percentage of non–German speakers are offline; yet scant government and social service information is available in languages other than German. Therefore segmented and specialized approaches are necessary to motivate them to use the Internet, approaches most likely to develop successfully in localities, with support from local, state, and national sources.

The targets of the Internet for All campaign in Germany mirror the groups identified as being on the wrong side of the digital divide in the U.S. government's 1999 report, "Falling through the Net." At the time, Assistant Secretary of Commerce Larry Irving called the issue of the digital divide a civil rights imperative for our times,[44] and the U.S. government leveraged its power to provoke widespread private-sector activity. Today the latest surveys on Internet use in the United States are not dissimilar from the German findings: 42 percent of Americans say they do not use the Internet, many either evading the technologies by having others navigate the tools for them or dropping out of cyberspace because of economic hardship or disillusionment.[45] The United States and Germany are surely not alone in experiencing a flattening of take-up and demand for services due not only to the deflationary economic climate but to the perceived lack of relevant content and curriculum meeting diverse information and communicative needs.

The German plan calls on the private sector to do its part in accelerating the diffusion of information and communications technologies in Germany. Unlike in the United States, where private-sector collaboration was decentralized (with the notable exception of the CEO Forum and a few other coordinated efforts), Chancellor Schröder attempted to cohere private-sector activities by chairing the Germany 21 Initiative [Deutschland 21] and offering companies a simple way to contribute. The ambitious goal of 20,000 long-term school sponsorships was established to improve computer and Internet use in the educational system, including a computer market for new and used PCs for schools;[46] only a fraction of these sponsorships came to pass. The D-21 sponsorship package included planning, installation, training, and maintenance in what the providers call a "no-worry packet" with the provision of lasting support and know-how.[47]

Following their respective national information society road maps, both countries witnessed significant increases in computer and Internet penetration in elementary and secondary schools. In terms of sheer diffusion, by early 2002, Germany reached twenty-three primary education students, seventeen secondary education students, and thirteen vocational education students per Internet-connected computer.[48] At the same time in the United States, there were six primary students and four secondary students per instructional computer connected to the Internet,[49] putting the United States on a par with Nordic countries and approximating the ratio some U.S. experts consider optimal from an educational viewpoint.[50]

The German federal initiative necessitated the sixteen state governments' developing their own complementary programs. Currently every state is running information society programs and Germany recently took up equipping schools. Since such an investment needs to be justified, the poorest and smallest of the German states, Bremen, embarked on a comprehensive approach to technology-infused learning called Web.Punkte.[51] Launched in the cities of Bremen and Bremerhaven with Deutsche Telekom, Web.Punkte is a two-year, €2 million experiment in twenty-five schools, opening their computer labs afternoons for students and community members. The initiative's main goal was to build bridges between schools and the larger community (e.g., developing cooperation among lifelong learning institutions), including attracting infrequent users such as immigrants and seniors. Students of diverse backgrounds from the Web.Punkte schools, moreover, were trained as "Web scouts," receiving certification as peer mentors to provide instruction to patrons. A preliminary evaluation describes a program exhibiting promise, with a need to expand cooperation with a larger network of learning and social service organizations to increase the visibility and the relevance of sites to community members.[52]

The U.S. Department of Education's Preparing Tomorrow's Teachers to Use Technology grant program (PT[3]) for several years supported high-quality reforms in teacher preparation programs for the purpose of increasing the knowledge, skills, and abilities of prospective teachers to use technology efficiently in their future teaching practices.[53] The program responded to the dilemma that elementary and secondary schools are now universally connected to the Internet, yet many teachers still feel uncomfortable using technology in their classrooms. The program was eliminated in 2002. A program in Germany to test the introduction of e-learning materials in everyday classrooms, called New Media in Education, is funded by the Federal Ministry of Education and Research. The use of new pedagogical methods—online teacher preparation, electronic portfolios, and Internet-based teacher programs—are all innovations to assist teachers if they have the time and support to absorb these approaches.

It is critical that innovative pedagogical or didactic practices and methodologies be supported, because intelligent computing and communications networks call for a robust learner-centered approach to education and instruction. In late 2002, the Bill and Melinda Gates Foundation funded the development of alternative upper-secondary schools for underachieving adolescents and young adults. Outside-the-box approaches were encouraged predicated on small class sizes and pervasive use of computing and networking to customize and extend the learning experience. Personalized approaches have been shown to enhance performance, and asynchronous extranets, linked with the broader community, can mitigate the inertia of socioeconomic disadvantage, creating virtual support networks and cooperative learning partnerships to assist students and their caregivers in their journeys as learners.[54]

The Finnish Model

At the end of 1998, the Ministry of Education in Finland set up a working group to prepare a proposal for a national strategy for education, training, and research in the information society for the years 2000–2004. This national strategy document is a sequel to the previous five-year plan adopted in 1994.[55] In the late 1990s, Finland devoted substantial resources to diffusing information and communications technologies in schools and other learning institutions, including modernizing a well-established library system.[56] The government's partnership with technology companies, including Nokia, to promote mobile communications as an educational tool, is promising. Since Finland has the highest mobile phone penetration in the world[57]—approaching the diffusion of color televisions sets—it may well become a bellwether among OECD countries in promoting portable, wireless tools to improve collaborative, around-the-clock learning.

Finland is one of the few OECD countries spending at least as much on training and research at the national level as on infrastructure.[58] In 1999 teaching techniques across universities and other educational institutions were heterogeneous, with only about one-fifth of educational staff applying computer networking extensively to support teaching.[59] Today the picture looks quite different. Since the Finnish Ministry of Education launched the Teacher Training Project (OPE.FI), over one-third of teachers have received advanced in-service training, according to Ritva-Sini Merilampi, counselor of education in the ministry. In terms of research and development, Finland is leveraging its competitive advantage in telecommunications applications to explore pervasive modes of lifelong learning in the information society[60] with an eye toward cooperative learning. Open-source tools are being tested in Finnish schools, and open learning environments are encouraged, expanding self-directedness, solidarity, teamwork, communications, and the possibilities of collective decision making in environments that flatten the distinctions between experts and laypeople.

Finland has achieved an overall high standard in its educational system and a high level of general education in the population, stemming from a national development strategy from the 1960s onward to create new universities all around the country. This policy, strongly linked with regional economic development and research, has sustained an egalitarian society with a high standard of living in which the information society and the welfare state manage to coexist relatively amicably.[61] Promoting a culture of lifelong learning, supported by strong links among diverse learning institutions (schools, libraries, workplaces, and homes) is a palpable vision. Education policy fosters a close contact with working life, a practice linked to increased retention rates and skills building among disadvantaged young people. The imperative also exists to build educational support structures extending throughout life, in part through the decompartmentalization of traditional learning arenas. Breaking down the separations between home, school, community, and work contributes to a deepening of learning opportunities beyond the confines of formal institutions and preset course offerings. Increasing parental involvement in young people's educational lives is a critical lever for amplifying learning by disadvantaged youths outside school walls. Expanding community accessibility to technology and training through libraries and after-school programs is also important, as is introducing youths to the working world.

Finland's commitment to equal educational opportunities so that no region or subgroup in the country lags behind others is a central component of its information society strategic action plan. With the near-universal diffusion of mobile phones in Finland, even in remote regions,[62] the emergent learning society fares well as mobile phones become the "central processing units" for information and communications exchange in the coming years. Computer and Internet access and use do tend to vary across regions in Finland, with a digital divide separating urban centers from rural areas, as well as along educational lines, with over 80 percent of Finns with a tertiary education using the Internet compared with under 50 percent of those with only a basic education.[63] But unlike in other countries, where lack of interest is a major barrier to Internet use, many Finns (with the exception of middle-aged and senior citizens in remote regions) say they do not require home connectivity because they have access on the job, at the neighborhood library, or at a nearby cybercafé.[64] These gaps appear less pronounced than in most other OECD countries, although a concerted effort to reach seniors and poor residents in remote areas of Finland remains a significant policy challenge.

In Finland student achievement tends to be relatively unvarying across geographical locations and economic strata,[65] suggesting that macro-level social and educational policies are fundamental in nurturing an egalitarian ethos. Indeed, the notion that information and communications technology diffusion and purposes tend to amplify preexisting institutional goals, strategies, and relationships appears to have merit in the instance of Finland, where regional development over several decades, coupled with rapid modernization of educational policy and practice, has generated a climate in which technology development broadly serves the needs of the population as a whole. This modus vivendi can be contrasted to those of Germany and the United States, where digital divides and achievement gaps are acute notwithstanding breakneck advances in technology diffusion.

Policy Implications

Four broad policy implications follow from the discussion of national information and communications technologies and education policymaking in the United States, Germany, and Finland. They can be summarized as follows. First, the vital importance of public- and private-sector leadership in developing and realizing information technology objectives cannot be underestimated, with an eye toward broad stakeholder involvement and a long-term vision for inclusion and excellence. Second, a focus on comprehensive and holistic approaches to technology integration is key. Too much fragmentation and superficiality in policymaking leads to inefficiency and benign neglect of the underlying causes of marginalization. Third, the importance of dependable and equitable funding streams to sustain and scale national initiatives is undeniable. Finally, human-capital development is the driver to raise performance and productivity for civic and economic inclusion.

In the late 1990s, OECD countries developed e-learning action plans, strongly supported by public- and private-sector leaders, to usher in the information society. This period's economic expansion allowed for unprecedented investments in infrastructure, digital content, and personnel training so that demonstrable productivity and learning gains began to occur. These huge sunken investments today have yielded a widespread digital infrastructure in many OECD countries, with broadband diffusion the new technological hurdle to cross vis-à-vis digital equity. This first wave of deep technology investments represents the end of the beginning, not the beginning of the end, both in renewing teaching and learning and in realizing significant efficiency and productivity gains from the tools. Indeed, the journey toward an equitable, high-performing Digital Nation is in its early stages. Standards for integrating digital literacy skills into most learning institutions' curricula and assessments have yet to be formed, let alone adopted, and teacher certification and professional support downplay technopedagogical innovation. Hence the need for robust leadership and vision lest the sunken investments contributing to closing the digital divide and the achievement gap wither on the vine.

In the United States several organizations and committees, including the CEO Forum on Education and Technology, a unique five-year partnership between business and education leaders, and the President's Information Technology Advisory Committee (PITAC), a panel of research, academic, and industry experts, offered recommendations on ways to unfurl a Digital Nation. Substantial expansion of equity provisions, professional development, and R&D were strongly endorsed under the mantle of a long-term investment strategy to increase educational technology funding as a proportion of the total education budget to 5 percent.[66] A new public-private coalition in the United States, the Partnership for 21st Century Skills, released a report establishing a common nomenclature and a readiness guide so schools can gauge their capacity to renew their teaching and learning using information and communications technologies. In the coming months and years, the coalition will deepen its work to influence the development of curricula and assessments as these tools truly become basic to learning in the twenty-first century.[67]

Action plans help to coordinate and steer national policy because the information society agenda cuts across many functional areas. In the United States almost every cabinet department has initiated e-developments; yet the sum total of these efforts are largely uncoordinated and offer weak links to the shrinking number of private-sector initiatives. The striking example from the United States is the E-rate, a program providing benefits to schools and libraries yet existing apart from the departments and agencies responsible for steering education and library policymaking. Without embedding technology into comprehensive, coordinated solutions to meet young people's real needs (with a strong role for research and evaluation), many benefits will remain unrealized.

With various ministries and departments motivated by different goals and accountability structures taking divergent approaches to an information society agenda, clearly there are gaps and redundancies in composing comprehensive solutions for underserved youths. Piecemeal approaches to content development, training, R&D, and infrastructure coverage will hinder countries in reaching their information society goals. According to the President's Information Technology Advisory Committee, "Education and learning R&D are dramatically underfunded," consisting of less than 0.1 percent of the total federal education budget.[68] PITAC recommended increasing this proportion to no less than 0.5 percent, or approximately $1.5 billion, in order to fund innovation in educational applications, such as virtual or mobile learning, digital content, and learning models customized to the needs of disadvantaged communities, such as the learning-disabled and immigrants.[69] This R&D, including rigorous evaluation of program effectiveness, should direct a country's strategic policy interventions, particularly on behalf of disadvantaged subgroups, to transcend the one-size-fits-all solutions often pervading a national policy agenda.

Clearly, developing human capital is the hallmark of an information society, including embarking on a process in which continuous learning opportunities are culturally acceptable and readily available. Beginning with teachers, infrequent opportunities exist to learn new skills in new environments. The CEO Forum recommended that the U.S. federal government should apply at least 30 percent of federal education technology funding to durable and intensive high-quality professional development by 2003; the actual investment today is much less.[70] Realizing an inclusive Digital Nation in this climate is an uphill climb. A culture of learning is also attenuated. U.S. adolescents spend upwards of 7 hours a day outside of school consuming media, mostly watching television and listening to music. And the video game craze has eclipsed Hollywood as a global commercial venture with uncertain social and physiological effects on children and adolescents. Redirecting young people's affinity for computing devices to more active and collaborative educational purposes will be a formidable challenge—and a fertile ground for R&D and potential policy intervention—in the years ahead.[71]

In the realm of technology equity, there is considerable room for stakeholder engagement. In fact, citizens will unlikely get the media environment receptive to the educational and social needs of young people on society's margins without raising their voices to be heard. The guideposts for a Digital Nation are still being established, and citizen engagement is essential, as well as strong leadership from governments, industry, and civil society. The message must be sent by concerned citizens—and well received by elected representatives—that a Digital Nation is for everyone, not just rhetorically but in concrete, sustained action in pursuit of its actualization. At a time when inequalities are growing in many OECD countries, information and communications technologies offer the potential to close achievement gaps and provide manifold opportunities for disadvantaged youths to enter the mainstream. But this will not happen without concerted attention and collective action toward creative solutions and bold new initiatives.

7

Wire-less Youth: Rejuvenating the Net

It is practically impossible to imagine a future that is not immersed in increasingly portable and minuscule information and communications devices. The "new kid on the block" in the 1990s, the Internet, is rapidly fading into the white noise of our daily experience, particularly for a younger generation, which Howe and Strauss call the Millennials, those born since 1982.[1]

According to the authors of *Millennials Rising,* this cohort bears little resemblance to Generation X, those born in the 1960s and 1970s. Millennials are more numerous, more affluent, better educated, and more ethnically diverse. Based on surveys, they describe themselves as not lost but found, born into an era when Americans are expressing more positive attitudes about children and young adults. They are also optimistic, upbeat about the world in which they are growing up. They are not selfish like the Me Generation but are team players. Importantly, they believe in the future, are engaged in civil society, and conceive themselves to be on the leading edge of progress, particularly when it comes to mastering new technologies.

Young people's potential for improving society, revitalizing our democracy, and ushering in a Digital Nation is confronted by the dominance of entertainment values and rapid consolidation in the media and telecommunications industries. Entertainment values, for example, are eclipsing the educational and civic dimensions of online activity. It is critical that this "can-do" generation participate in reinventing the medium to improve people's lives, particularly in an increasingly global context. While the Internet is becoming second nature for many young people, new forms of online civic practice need to ferment and expand to fulfill its full potential as an empowering medium.

The Future Is Here, and It's for Sale

Millennials are used to "multitasking," to employing many types of technology all at once, for example, instant-messaging friends while doing homework, talking on the phone while watching television or listening to music. Many teenagers have their own Web sites—their own digital soapboxes—and are generally more adept users of technology than their parents, a majority of whom still rely on snail mail to keep in touch.

On a typical day, Millennials will spend about 6½ hours using media—watching television, listening to music, reading and working on the computer, and meeting new e-pals, often halfway around the world.[2] What we know, as the great media theorist Marshall McLuhan suggested two generations ago, is that in general people use new media to supplement, not replace, older forms of media. For now, teenagers who spend a lot of time with computers also watch more TV and read more than most others.

Within this media environment, digital technologies and online activities are increasingly occupying youths' attention. E-mail, instant messaging, and chat groups are incredibly popular among teens, as are downloading music files and buying products online. Among 18- and 19-year-olds, 91 percent use e-mail and 83 percent use instant messaging, with 56 percent of older teens saying they prefer the Internet to the telephone.[3] With the acceleration of high-speed Internet connections over cable and next-generation wireless tools, where youths are able to color-coordinate and personalize their communications devices, these numbers and the time youths spend online will in all likelihood increase.

This digital landscape is not altogether rosy because many new applications and gizmos under development are geared toward amusement rather than education and engagement. Commercials for high-speed Internet service and faster microprocessors tout the entertainment value of these advances. In Intel ads, for example, sepia-toned aliens learn to use the Pentium-4 processor to play more lifelike video games and to download multimedia entertainment. High-speed broadband services are being marketed as delivery mechanisms for movies-on-demand and interactive video games. Who will deliver health care online or expand distance education opportunities?

The video game industry is just one example of how entertainment values are eclipsing demand for noncommercial content. In 2000 sales of hardware and software for interactive games eclipsed Hollywood for the first time, with sales totaling $8.2 billion, versus $7.75 billion in U.S. movie box office receipts.[4] There are thousands of titles, many of which are overly violent. Despite the huge market and the relatively high penetration of video-gaming consoles in underserved communities (e.g., Microsoft's Xbox and Sony's Playstation), hardly anyone is creating marketable educational content, let alone applications for youths to plug into what's going on in their neighborhoods. As these consoles become more sophisticated and allow young people to connect with gaming partners online, it will be critical to develop educational and civic content, such as variations on the popular SimCity; otherwise, the online experience will become just another diversion for our children. Parents and educators must demand this content, and government must create public venture funds to experiment with socially beneficial applications.

Entertainment applications may be what drive the market, but public and private (philanthropic) funders of technology and media content should devote substantial resources to public media, that is, enterprises that develop the noncommercial, democratic components of digital media. Additionally, public-media partnerships, such as those between broadcasting stations and community groups, need to focus on fostering a diversity of voices at the local level: underserved young people become an important target to develop their ability to express their aspirations through new media. While young adults are least likely to vote of any age group, their enthusiasm for new technologies might be just the lever to encourage more young adults to exercise their franchise. The Markle Foundation in New York City is among the only private philanthropies investing in socially beneficial interactive applications aimed at children. But the scope of the investments is too small to affect the marketplace noticeably. What is needed is substantial public funding for public-media content and robust leadership to make the case that these investments are worthwhile. These dollars need to build the capacity of communities to be producers of their own content, not just passive consumers of prepackaged fare. A credible proposal is circulating in Congress to use the proceeds from spectrum auctions to fund these programs.

One example of a program that brings community groups together with media producers to enhance engagement in the larger community is the Benton Foundation's Sound Partners for Community Health,[5] a partnership with the Robert Wood Johnson Foundation. The program fosters creative solutions to health care problems by linking community organizations with public radio stations to produce programming that addresses local needs. Sound Partners supports sixty-eight partnerships in the United States to demonstrate the civic role that broadcasters and community organizations can play in local communities. The program amplifies the voices of underserved communities, as illustrated by a partnership between KUAC-FM and Native American youths in Fairbanks, Alaska, in which youths are trained with digital media to undertake a dialogue with listeners about substance abuse and recovery.

Replicating this program through other platforms, such as satellite radio or Webcasting, would lower the cost and expand the scope of what's possible within these budding partnerships. Young people are receptive to these civic activities and partnerships because they are invited to connect with their community on their own terms, by using media about which they are already excited to tap into issues of relevance to their everyday lives.

A Generation, Divided

In order for communities to play a leading role in working with media partners to produce programming and content of value, the digital literacy skills of community members, particularly young people, must be more fully developed. The term *digital literacy* captures the types of capacities that need to be cultivated so that communities can effectively use computer applications, video, and Internet tools to improve their lives. Perhaps the highest-order digital literacy is for citizens to be media producers, not just passive consumers, to use available outlets to voice their hopes and concerns, to be citizen-producers. For this to happen, widespread access to digital media is critical as well as the training and mentoring to cultivate young people's talents. Notwithstanding the fact that many young people are Internet savvy—often more so than their parents and teachers—significant digital divides exist in access and training, particularly acute in high-poverty and rural communities, at a time when retrenchment in national leadership in combating this problem signals a decline in funding and resources to develop locally driven content more fully.

Two giant media companies, AOL Time Warner and Bertelsmann, convened a conference in Berlin in March 2002 on twenty-first-century literacy. World leaders such as German Chancellor Gerhard Schröder and Madeleine Albright, Secretary of State in the Clinton administration, spoke of the power and promise of information and communications technologies to knock down walls, very appropriate given Berlin's recent history. Chancellor Schröder asserted that digital literacy should now take its place as a basic literacy alongside reading, writing, and arithmetic, recognizing the pivotal role of information and communications technologies in underwriting lifelong learning, economic productivity, and democratic engagement. Given Europe's aging population, policy leaders there recognize that it is critical to enhance productivity substantially among younger workers to sustain the quality of life to which Europeans are accustomed.

The twenty-first-century literacy conference was hosted under the shadow of the Brandenberg Gate, the symbol of a city at the center of former political strife. At the time of the conference, the edifice was shrouded under a drop cloth, undergoing restoration and renewal. Since Deutsche Telekom is supporting the renovation project, the company took the opportunity to use the gate as a giant advertisement for its Internet service, called T-Online. The slogan brandished across the famous landmark declares that "Im Internet ist alles möglich"—everything is possible with the Internet.

Widespread enthusiasm over the future of society immersed in technology prevails after the dot-com bubble burst and in the post-9/11 environment. Millennials lead the charge. And the potential is enormous. Yet this excitement continues to cover over the forms of social and economic exclusion that exist in the United States and Europe, and between developed and developing nations.[6] Juxtaposed with the reality of poverty and underdevelopment in technology infrastructure, the Deutsche Telekom banner is ironic, symbolizing not only the hopes but also the unfulfilled potential that requires our collective action to realize fully.

With over 1 billion people in the world between the ages of 15 and 24, improving livelihoods and creating jobs are central challenges, ones that smart use of information and communications technologies may help turn into digital opportunities. The challenges are immense, given that 80 percent of the world's population has yet to make a phone call and a majority of young people live in developing countries where there is often little opportunity for productive work. And to tear down the walls of economic exclusion, we need to create markets to raise standards of living in communities outside the bounds of global trade, or poverty will continue to sow the seeds of animosity and envy between haves and have-nots. The Education Development Center in Boston has teamed with the World Bank to work with youths from five developing countries to initiate business plans for renewable energy enterprises, creating employment opportunities while also tackling environmental degradation. These efforts need to multiply and be supported by investments both in youth leadership and in strengthening the organizational capacity of youth-serving institutions.

In the United States social exclusion and alienation persist, whether in South Boston or in the tribal lands of the western United States, where communities continue to languish without basic information and communications infrastructure. High dropout rates and lack of preparedness for employment in today's economy deepen social exclusion. At the end of 2001, only about 14 percent of children living in low-income families were using the Internet at home compared with 63 percent of children in families earning over $75,000 per year.[7] With respect to race and ethnicity, as figure 7.1 reveals, 50 percent of non-Hispanic white children and 52 percent of Asian children used the Internet at home in 2001 compared with only 25 percent of African-American children and 20 percent of Hispanics. Many underserved youths also attend public schools with little access to and effective integration of emerging technologies, a missed opportunity given what we know about the positive effects of virtual learning environments in improving the motivation and performance of at-risk teenagers. Minority-serving institutions, such as tribal colleges and historically black colleges, can only dream of doing what America's elite colleges and universities have accomplished, given the gap in resources.

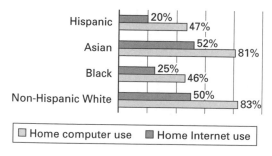

Figure 7.1
Home Computer and Internet Use among Children, 2001
Source: Wilhelm, Carmen, and Reynolds (2002).

Although the federal government and leading private-sector companies have spent billions of dollars in recent years to improve access to and effective use of computers and the Internet in schools and libraries, there are signs that this commitment is slowing in the wake of economic insecurity and a change of priorities at the top levels of government. Companies that invested heavily in educational technology initiatives, such as Cisco and Lucent, are pulling the plug or scaling back their investments. And the federal government is also scuttling programs aimed at building technology capacity in communities, training teachers, and demonstrating technology applications, such as e-government and telemedicine, in underserved communities.

So, "the future is here—it's just not equally distributed."[8] Without access to these tools as well as the ability to use them effectively, we are missing a necessary link in jump-starting and sustaining global educational, economic, and civic advances aimed at the nearly 1 billion teenagers and young adults in the developed and developing worlds.

Youths as Producers and Savvy Consumers

Millennials see themselves on the cutting edge of something new. This society and culture in which communications tools are pervasive is second nature for many young adults. Indeed, they themselves are actors and cocreators in its unfolding—both as consumers and as producers of new content and applications—the very essence of twenty-first-century literacy. Although digital information and communications technologies are consolidating in the hands of a few media conglomerates, the media landscape is far from bleak.

Teenage and young adult consumers are increasingly targets of corporations, with 32 million teens accounting for $172 billion in spending money in 2001, half of them now shopping online.[9] ABC Network's attempt to replace *Nightline* with David Letterman's *Late Show* in order to attract advertisers for the young adult niche market underscores this reality.

As consumers, youths have significant economic and political power, for instance, in promoting "green" products and supporting fair labor practices across the globe. In the 1980s *institutions* used their clout to pressure social and political change, for example, through divesting financial holdings in South Africa. Yet today *individuals* are exercising their power as consumers (as critical market segments or niches) and investors (e.g., through socially responsible investments) to influence market behavior. For young people, consumer behavior is tantamount to a political act. A Marymount University poll of one thousand adults revealed that 75 percent of consumers would avoid shopping at stores that sell sweatshop-made clothes. But, of course, it is critical to know who the worst perpetrators are, and then youths must organize and engage decision makers to act on this information. Undoubtedly, the role of the Internet and other digital technologies is pivotal.

Most important, youths are not just consumers but also producers, riding the crest of the wave of innovation and new practices that have blossomed in the past decade. Because youths have facility with these tools, they have the potential to shape the emerging Digital Nation for social good.

The power of the Internet and other digital media resides in their interactivity, the ability of users to be producers, not just passive recipients as with one-way broadcast media. The Internet is also an effective organizing tool, enabling communities of interest across the globe to broaden the scope of involvement and engagement in their issues at relatively low transaction costs. Finally, to be an Internet publisher, a low-power radio producer, or a wi-fi operator, start-up costs are substantially lower than those in traditional, saturated media such as broadcast, allowing young people in basements or community centers to hurdle entry barriers and become global digital denizens.

The young entrepreneur Omar Wasow, who directly upon graduating from Stanford University founded New York Online, a cyber-community of New Yorkers from all walks of life, is now the architect of BlackPlanet, a Web portal that brings the worldwide African diaspora together into an online community that allows members to cultivate personal and professional relationships, gain access to relevant goods and services, and stay informed about and engaged in the larger world.[10]

On a larger scale, the Intel Corporation has created the Intel Computer Clubhouse, a model that uses technology creatively to enable inner-city youths to acquire the tools, problem-solving skills, and confidence necessary for successful lives. In partnership with the Museum of Science, Boston, its award-winning Computer Clubhouse, and the MIT Media Lab, Intel is supporting the establishment of one hundred Intel Computer Clubhouses in low-income communities worldwide. The Clubhouse is exporting a model of how youths should interact with technology and their society through active engagement, a learning philosophy embedded in the constructivist theories of Seymour Papert.

On a smaller scale and on an ad hoc basis, this exciting mix of youths' enthusiasm for creating and designing, coupled with the possibilities inherent in the technologies, has generated partnerships at the grassroots level across the United States and globally. An initiative in Chicago called Street-Level Youth Media works with inner-city youths in media arts and emerging technologies for use in self-expression, communications, and social change. In developing forms of expression and journalism with new media from the point of view of young people and their concerns, Street-Level Youth Media provides a platform for the larger community to hear from youths in their own voice rather than through the lens of mainstream media and its often negative depictions of youths. In sharp contrast to these messages, what is often revealed through youth media is an abiding concern for neighborhood, identity, and global justice. Through the power of interactive media, when youths are put in charge, what is revealed is the exercise of a latent desire for political engagement, using media to connect with the world and to cut across traditional borders of geography and identity.

Unlike the diffusion of prior communications tools, new media are being driven partly by the use patterns of teenagers and young adults who are shaping what remains a budding social practice. With the rollout of print in the fifteenth century or the telegraph in the nineteenth century, the role of young people was peripheral at best. With the commercial Internet only fifteen hundred days old, clearly there is a primary role for youths to lead as early adopters and shapers of this medium.

Millennials Go Global

Surveys show that Millennials are team-oriented and are engaged in community service, volunteering, and efforts to improve the environment, reflecting a keen interest in the unfolding global civil society. Youths are eager to embrace unpopular causes and support the underdog in battles for global justice, such as support for the plight of indigenous peoples. The elders of the Mirrar clan of Australia, for example, began fighting the establishment of new uranium mining within their territory and have since been joined by scores of Australian youths who embrace the justice of their cause. With the Internet, youths can seize the opportunity to reach out and extend their own sense of global identity and responsibility as they reinvent community building for the twenty-first century.

No example better highlights this commitment than the World Trade Organization (WTO) process, in particular the meetings in Seattle in 1999. At this event, ministers and industrialists convened to discuss the best arrangements to buttress world free trade while, unbeknownst to them, student, labor, and nonprofit groups were using the power of the Internet to organize to counteract this trend. A photo taken by a *Seattle Times* reporter during the protests best captured the tension, showing an arrow pointing in one direction for the WTO decision-making process and in the opposite direction for democracy, democratic self-determination in the minds of the protesters having been undermined by its closed-door format.

Another phenomenon that demands the engagement of youths relates to the worldwide rise in racism, xenophobia, and violence against immigrants, particularly those of Arabic descent, emerging in the wake of the war on terror. September 11 is likely to be a political flashpoint in young people's lives, similar in effect to the assassination of John F. Kennedy for the boomer generation. How youths respond to this challenge will likely shape the future of U.S. relations vis-à-vis the rest of the world. In the United States and Europe, anti-immigrant platforms and parties continue to gain ground, and state-sponsored violence has expanded in the name of quashing disempowered groups branded as terrorists.

To diffuse these parties of intolerance, and to begin to hurdle the barriers that separate religious, ethnic, racial, and cultural groups in society, it is critical that youths harness the power of the Internet to cultivate a more tolerant and inclusive world. Government, philanthropy, business, and educational communities, among others, should be in the forefront of experimenting with communications technology in the post-9/11 environment to promote understanding and rapprochement between cultures while at the same time, through this example, encouraging free and flourishing civil societies, including the empowerment of women, especially in the Middle East, which is the focus of the current preoccupation with terrorism.

Opening up to the wider world through seamless Web offerings, such as ongoing electronic conferencing and transorganizational content development would favor mutual knowledge and understanding. One idea might be to reach out to youth organizations and learning institutions in the Middle East to cultivate an interest in using the new media to explore mutual understanding, both culturally and in ascertaining the impact of the technology on civil relations. The potential for cross-cultural dialogue and cooperation among teenagers and young adults could be stimulating.

The surge of different forms of radicalism and intolerance reveals the deficit of dialogue and understanding between cultures, not to mention symptoms of growing economic inequalities between rich and poor. Face-to-face exchange (e.g., expanding study-abroad programs) and transnational public works projects, complemented and extended with communications technologies such as e-mail and conferencing, may just transform attitudes by allowing younger generations to compare their respective national values and cultures, while deepening this emerging internationalism already percolating among Millennials.

What's My Age in Web Years?

What we know is that youths care deeply about their communities and about social justice, and if motivated and empowered can rejuvenate the forms of civic practice prevalent on the Web today. As the poet Emily Brontë wrote as a young adult, the aspirations of youths can often be obscured:

Sweet love of youth, forgive, if I forget thee,
While the world's tide is bearing me along;
Other desires and other hopes beset me,
Hopes which obscure, but cannot do thee wrong![11]

Yet with new technology, the desires and hopes of youths can be channeled into exciting new practice. Based on my own observations and study of Internet conversation, outlined in my book *Democracy in the Digital Age,* several trends have emerged that obscure, but hopefully will not eclipse, promising forms of cross-cultural dialogue and forums for democratic problem solving online.

The first challenge centers on providing information versus information seeking. Particularly when it comes to political chat, participants are more than eager to chime in and express their points of view and substantially less likely to make requests to fill gaps or seek exploration of alternative views on issues about which they are interested. While self-expression is clearly important, youths need to listen to each other and to decision makers, entering into dialogue in order to broach understanding and act collectively in the light of day. Types of civic journalism and new media production, in encouraging youths to find the most marginal voices in community and give them the microphone, promote the value, fundamental to a democracy, that all voices, not just the powerful, can be heard. In New York City, HarlemLive, a youth Internet publication, recently provided a platform on their Web site for young Palestinian refugees to speak about their daily lives under occupation, so that we can listen and understand, unfettered and uninterrupted.

Second, there is a tendency with information and communications technologies, and the straw polls and plebiscite-like activity rampant on commercial portals, to want to register individual preferences and then aggregate them rather than encouraging exchange and thoughtful response to discussion threads. We should move away from aggregating preferences and look toward fostering common ground and illuminating and reconciling points of contention that require continuing discussion, debate, and elaboration. People need to feel responsible before other community members so that citizens and community members become more than a fraction of a passive, consumer public. The international human rights and development portal, OneWorld.net, possesses an exciting feature called OneWorld TV in which anybody around the globe can post video footage representing their point of view on social issues, clips other users can add to, comment on, or use openly for instructional or other purposes, a true global marketplace of ideas.

Finally, through chat groups and online discussion forums, participants tend to gravitate toward like-minded individuals so that cyberspace largely becomes an extension of the social networks and hobby groups one would join and belong to in a physical community. What does this homogeneity imply for overcoming difference, encouraging tolerance and understanding as well as broadening our horizons, particularly given the global possibilities of these technologies?

Of course, the architecture of a network or online discussion, including its functionality, along with the presence of expert moderation, will affect the quality of online exchange, and new software ought to be reviewed and tested to increase the quality of online discussion.

Clearly, there are many technological hurdles, and technology continues to change so rapidly that it is sometimes hard to keep pace with the latest device or tool. But these are only tools. The great challenge on the horizon in the twenty-first century is a social, not a technological, one, that is to say, coming to terms with our diversity in a Digital Nation. Encouraging a diversity of viewpoints and cultures ought to be the hallmark of a liberal society, and the technological innovations and digitally mediated social practices brokered by young people hopefully will bring us closer to an inclusive global civil society that honors diversity.

Conclusion

Beginning this book, I offered Freud's analysis of the three primary sources of human discontent as one framework to begin to comprehend the nature and scope of technology's role in history's unfolding. In depicting our struggles with nature, the deterioration of our bodies, and social conflict as the central conditions confronting humanity over the ages, Freud painted a stark picture of a world torn asunder by internecine strife and ravaged by natural disaster, all this while grappling with the psychology of human mortality.[1] Other luminaries, such as John Stuart Mill, saw in our mastery of nature the unleashing of previously unimaginable productive forces to liberate and empower humanity. With his Victorian looking-glass, Mill surveyed invention and discovery promising to unburden a laboring humanity, especially the working classes.[2] For Mill, as for John Rawls one hundred years later, the challenge was not so much the mastery of nature but rather the fair distribution and civilized use of the fruits of our mastery.[3] For Freud, civilization was a veneer, barely masking our barbaric nature. But for Mill and Rawls, people were capable of living commodiously under the right circumstances of solidarity, democracy, and equality.

Injustice translates generally into social unrest as the social basis for self-respect and solidarity is unrealizable under conditions of stark inequality. Over long stretches of human history, the fates of human societies often hinged on the possession and wise control of technologies, including their use, intended or otherwise, to engineer new social opportunity. The possession of guns and steel obviously gave advantages to Europe and America over the past several centuries. But the benefits of modern industrialization, in terms of unparalleled social advances, came at a high price with the horror of colonial subjugation and industrial exploitation. Technology diffusion has often played a pivotal role in the rise and fall of civilizations over the millennia. As Jared Diamond tells us, "When a widely useful invention does crop up in one society, it then tends to spread in either of two ways. One way is that other societies see or learn of the invention, are receptive to it, and adopt it. The second is that societies lacking the invention find themselves at a disadvantage vis-à-vis the inventing society, and they become overwhelmed and replaced if the disadvantage is sufficiently great."[4]

The threat of information and communications technologies creating massive advantages for some societies and regions, and perhaps contributing to the demise of others, follows a long line of relatively recent inventions—the locomotive, electrification, the automobile—that spawned modern metropolises and unrivaled economic productivity while also leading to the disappearance of other places and ways of life. At a national or regional level, entities vie to sharpen their competitive advantages in a rapidly globalizing political economy as the repercussions of falling behind technologically translate into draining brainpower, eroding foreign investment, and declining quality of life, a confluence of factors perhaps dealing certain communities a final coup de grâce. Countries often respond overwhelmingly when they believe their competitive advantage is eroding and their way of life is at risk, such as the United States during the so-called space race or in response to the perceived Japanese economic juggernaut of the 1980s, or Germany after the release of the 2000 international student assessment scores (PISA). After it was revealed that German students' skills and knowledge proficiencies ranked poorly relative to other industrialized countries, the federal government responded, plowing €4 billion into a new program to extend the school day in order to shore up a failing academic regimen.

Countries going digital perceive they will have an edge over their competitors, so that a Digital Nation becomes the latest beacon of preeminence in the unfolding of human ingenuity put to productive purposes. To lag in the diffusion of information and communications tools can be lethal for regions and countries already outside the flow of financial capital and underdeveloped in terms of basic indicators of well-being, such as education and health. What vanishes, perhaps as quickly and decisively as the carrier pigeon, is not just economic activity but cultural identity, as human diversity is leached in the uneven exchange of cultural symbols and wares through the concentrated media and technology industries. Analogous to

Darwin's theory of species evolution, it is at least possible in a milieu in which cultural diversity is impoverished that social evolution is also endangered, as the errant idea or dissenting theory is less likely to be born, ideas leading potentially to the next cure or the decisive counterpoint to the wornness of received opinion. In his classic statement of freedom of thought and opinion, John Stuart Mill tells us that "only through diversity of opinion is there, in the existing state of human intellect, a chance of fair play to all sides of the truth."[5]

Since so much is at stake, it is imperative that countries and regions step up their efforts to migrate to cyberspace. The digital race in space is very real; but critical advantage is not found in gaining the higher ground in the military sense or in having centralized control of information and intelligence. Missiles in space, defense shields, centralized information databases, surveillance tools, and strictures on the flow of money and ideas are artifacts of a nefarious culture of control out of joint with the temper of post-Enlightenment living and the civilized aspirations of human communities. Centralized control is a chimera in an age of networked intelligence in which the forces of centralization—government, military, and corporate—struggle to maintain their grip on the flow of ideas, people, and money, as tenable a hold in the long run as the capture of sand in a sieve.

Democratic, legitimate Digital Nations in the twenty-first century will use the potential of networked intelligence and the promise of decentralization as the primary arterials for human empowerment and liberation. Countries such as Finland tap the power of information technologies to broaden and deepen the connections within and among regional economic and community development zones. Even in sparsely populated areas of the country, the strategy is to link a critical mass of institutions, usually with a university serving as an anchor tenant, to foster lifelong learning and business incubation, always building on indigenous cultural and social assets. This said, Finns are not enamored of technology and are firmly antideterministic. Information and communications technologies are tools to be fashioned to meet people's educational, business, and social needs and goals, including sparking the light of self-investigation and discovery in every Finn—young or old, rich or poor, urban or rural, immigrant or indigenous—to fulfill individual and collective life goals.

Achieving a Digital Nation will require charismatic leadership and a critical mass of bottom-up support in order to recruit the political allies to muster the necessary budget outlays. Leadership must be able to translate to a wide constituency why a Digital Nation is paramount. Drilling down to people's everyday realities, leaders must build grassroots support to recruit new allies to the nascent movement, for example, articulating to parents why they should buy a computer for their kids, or lobbying school boards to support extra professional development to build digital literacy in a fresh cadre of teachers. At the macro level, the imperative of national comparative advantage should mobilize politicians and industry leaders to promote next-generation Digital Nation policies while not losing sight of the fact that inclusion in the digital age is a categorical imperative. From a self-interest point of view, politicians desire to reach voters with their message and can do so more cheaply and widely if citizens are online and using the Internet. Industry, too, needs help in tapping new markets, particularly since many companies have overinvested in infrastructure capacity relative to the customers they have wooed in a contracting economic climate. Building on the self-interest of politicians and business, as well as the legal obligation of governments to serve their residents, will avoid this issue's becoming a civil rights struggle in the coming era.

A Digital Nation political platform also bids public figures and those in civil society to reform outworn approaches to social problems, many of which have reached an impasse: skyrocketing health care costs and out-of-control urban congestion and sprawl are symptomatic, threatening future economic prosperity and quality of life. Technology does not provide a final answer but rather an invitation to reinvigorate our thinking in approaching stalemated issues, hopefully to tackle them more systemically and holistically. For example, can we explore low-cost strategies to extend e-health benefits, such as diagnosis, hospice, monitoring, and access to clinical specialists to indigent Americans, particularly those outside of the health care system? How can we mitigate rush-hour congestion in metropolitan regions with e-work and intelligent use of information and communications technologies to alleviate and to regulate arterial flow?

Public education and awareness raising are critical to nudge public behavior in the direction of becoming facile with new technologies, building skills and knowledge to function in a Digital Nation. Messages advocating environmentally friendly behavior and healthy life choices have proven effective, and public campaigns tailored to local learning systems would be particularly useful, perhaps leading residents to specific neighborhood computer centers or libraries where they can use a computer, take a class, or look for a job. Linking the ads to building a stronger learning culture would be useful, suggesting it is "cool" to be connected to the Internet and to use one's leisure time to be learning. After all, a lifetime of adaptability and retooling will be the norm in the new economy, forcing people to be nimble. Portable communications devices and computers will increasingly provide the gateway to learning. For residents completely marginalized from the computer culture, neighborhood fairs and demonstrations in shopping centers and church basements might offer exposure as well as tips on how to buy or finance computing devices.

This kind of local barn raising is not sufficient, as effective as it is in generating grassroots interest in a course of action for a community. Clear and achievable national goals and benchmarks must also be articulated so that unhindered pathways can serve to steer national resources effectively. Hitching our wagons to more ambitious broadband rollout and tougher requirements for technology literacy in schools, both for students and teachers, are only feasible if leadership formulates deft policy designs, with clear goals, including incentives and penalties for noncompliance, and then rallies the political will to support these endeavors financially. A Digital Nation cannot rise like a phoenix from the ashes of inaction and indifference on the part of government and business leadership. Without vision from local and national opinion shapers, communities will sputter along until they become marginal and obsolete, and the future will continue to lack meaning for too many people.

In leading information societies, technology is not cordoned off and isolated from core functional social arenas; rather, it is integrated into strategies to enable advances in education, improvement in health, engagement in civil society and economic life. In short, a Digital Nation is much more than industrial policy; it drives the social agenda as information, skills, and knowledge become building blocks of a learning culture. Connecting the dots among programs and departments already engaged in building a Digital Nation—in education, labor, human services, commerce, energy, and transportation—ought to be the job of a high-ranking public individual. The job would entail not just leveraging extant programs, teasing out how programs might be "e-enabled," but would focus on the prospective advantages of information and communications technologies in doing things differently, not just faster and cheaper. More than a chief information officer, a technocrat working on software interoperability, the liaison would explore substantive, forward-looking partnerships across government. In this way, the function would resemble the U.K. Office of the e-Envoy, charged with leading the drive to get the United Kingdom online. The liaison would also need a budget to commission action research similar to the work done at the Institute for Prospective Technology Studies in Seville, Spain, which provides expert policy-relevant research and analysis for policymakers on the relationship between technology, the economy, and society.

Embodied in the new liaison role would be four key functions. First, the liaison would assist in coordinating and leveraging existing projects, including seeking strategic partnerships with localities, businesses, and nongovernmental organizations. Strengthening the relationship between the fields of community technology and economic development, for example, might lead to fruitful synergies between ed-tech and empowerment-zone resources, with schools and nonprofits serving as anchor tenants for job training, skill development, and community building. Second, the liaison would serve a critical public relations role, spearheading popular campaigns, conducting town hall meetings, and raising the visibility of a Digital Nation agenda before the people. Third, the liaison would be the champion of a Digital Nation platform within government. Since these issues often do not receive the priority they deserve in public agenda setting, the liaison would kindle interest and engagement among politicians. The liaison would also link with designated point people within key departments to form a Digital Nation roundtable meeting regularly for interagency collaboration. Finally, the liaison would commission research and development, exploring next-generation information and communications technologies and their potential role in shaping economic and social life. This long-term perspective is critical, given that governments often cannot see past the next election cycle.

Any commitment to a Digital Nation agenda that pays more than lip service to the ambitious slate of issues on the table requires dependable and equitable funding. Rather than relying on nonrecurring grants, usually with program funding cobbled together between these and reallocated operating budgets, schools, nonprofit organizations, hospitals, and other organizations require sustained funding streams or multiyear grant awards to fund training, content, infrastructure investments and modernization as well as institutional support to build internal capacity to use these tools effectively. This agenda is too important to rely exclusively on private philanthropy or the private sector.

During heated negotiations leading up to the passage of the 1996 Telecommunications Act, corporations wanted regulatory forbearance from government in exchange for their cooperation in collecting funds for a new universal service program, the E-rate. While the fees are derived from consumers, not corporate revenues, politicians and corporations have tried to scuttle the program, under various pretenses. Other corporate groups, such as the broadcasters, have reneged on their obligation to serve the public interest. An array of companies providing information services, such as Internet providers, are largely unbridled and resist the imposition of common-carrier obligations or public-interest standards which regulate other industry segments. Rather than seeking to alter corporate behavior to produce more children's programming or to collect universal service fees, policymakers should focus their energies on giving communities the tools to empower themselves, so they can ultimately demand more from the media culture or create their own alternative media. Commercial broadcasters, for example, should be able to opt out of their public-interest obligations for a fee, to be ploughed into noncommercial media alliances, local content creation, and other community capacity building.[6]

Action is needed from the U.S. Congress to establish a fund to address the key challenges of achieving a Digital Nation. The fund could be derived from various sources, and the strategy for how best to move legislation in support of a Digital Nation trust fund will depend on political exigencies. For example, a bill currently before Congress proposes to take the proceeds from spectrum auctions to fund the transition from analog to digital. Yet these monies are already earmarked to ease the skyrocketing national deficit or to militarize the electromagnetic spectrum. So, further strategizing on the part of public-interest groups must be part of a Digital Nation grassroots movement to build public pressure for congressional action.

The first goal of a Digital Nation is to achieve universal service to the information services, computing devices, and communications networks all people need for economic gain and civic engagement. Rather than a one-size-fits-all universal service policy like the one that underwrites telephone service, people ought to be given a menu of choices to best meet their information and communications needs.[7] In addition to ensuring universal home access to the essential information and communications tools of the day, existing and new grant programs ought to be expanded to spark experimentation in schools, libraries, community centers, and other learning institutions, such as the widespread use of community-based mobile learning to address the educational needs of young people and adults.

The second goal is to build on the one-dimensional approach exemplified by overinvestment in hardware by fully funding training, content development, and new applications. The extent to which people are trained to use information and communications technologies effectively will determine to a large degree the level of success achieved in migrating the nation to cyberspace. New content and curriculum, especially educational materials and local information sources, will likely not emerge from the private sector, so they must be supported more robustly through public spending. And applications that begin to test the new frontiers of digital media, such as customized devices for diverse learning styles, virtual schools, and intelligent tutorials, require an accelerated commitment to research and development, experimentation, and innovation between public and private partners. Education is the killer app of the twenty-first century and should be a top-tier priority for governments, business, and communities, particularly in enhancing lifelong learning opportunities through innovative uses of networking and computing tools. Rather than supporting a retrograde back-to-basics approach, leadership ought to shape a compelling vision for democratic, open learning spaces, virtual and otherwise, using technology appropriately to customize anytime, anywhere content, curricula, and activities for people of all ages and walks of life.

In the end a Digital Nation must be a reflection of a democratic society having harnessed the best technology can offer in pursuit of the well-being and edification of its people. The interactive, asynchronous, and portable attributes of the new technologies offer a compelling invitation to reform and revamp outworn institutions and organizations, creating avenues for deeper participation and accountability. Incentives are needed in the form of multiyear grants to consortia of community organizations to begin to reshape how services are delivered and what counts as education in the swift currents of a Digital Nation. Navigating this society will require that people be motivated and empowered to invent their own futures, buoyed by a new social contract in which rampant inequalities sown by the acquisitive spirit are tempered by the tender embrace of liberty, equality, and solidarity.

Notes

Chapter 1

1. Freud (1930), 25.

2. Elliott (2003).

3. Berkowitz (2003).

4. Ravitz, Becker, and Wong (2000), 7–8.

5. "Education is not the filling of a pail but the lighting of a fire." Attributed to W. B. Yeats.

6. <http://www.infocentros.org.sv/> [Spanish]; <http://home.pacbell.net/nmolina/el_salvador.htm> [Google offers an English translation, including the <http://www.infocentros.org.sv/> site.]

7. "State Promotes Jobs Web Site Where Few People Use Computers," *Birmingham News,* November 29, 2002.

8. VISTAS (Visually Impaired Specialized Training and Advocacy Services). <http://www.vistascenter.org/aboutus.htm>.

9. Chow et al. (1998), 23–24.

10. Universal Service Administrative Company (2003), 4–5.

11. "Telecommunications Act of 1996," § 254.

12. Sum, Fogg, and Mangum (2000), 23.

13. Krueger and Lindahl (2001), 1101.

14. Krueger (1991), 7.

15. Litan and Rivlin, eds. (2002), 21.

16. Kirsch et al. (2002), 100.

17. Donahue et al. (2001), 31.

18. Speech, Telecom 99: Eighth World Telecommunications Exhibition and Forum, Geneva, October 1999.

19. "[Powell] then added that he thought 'digital divide' was a dangerous phrase because it could be used to justify government entitlement programs that guaranteed poor people cheaper access to new technology, like digital television sets or

computers. . . . 'I think there is a Mercedes divide,' he said. 'I'd like to have one; I can't afford one. I'm not meaning to be completely flip about this. I think it's an important social issue. But it shouldn't be used to justify the notion of essentially the socialization of the deployment of the infrastructure.' " Stephen Labaton, "New F.C.C. Chief Would Curb Agency Reach," *New York Times,* February 7, 2001.

20. Grossman and Minow (2001), 15ff.

21. A public education campaign sponsored by the Kaiser Family Foundation, AOL Time Warner, the American Library Association, the Leadership Conference on Civil Rights, and the Benton Foundation. The database of community technology centers underlying the campaign is maintained by the Digital Divide Network (<http://www.digitaldividenetwork.org/content/sections/index.cfm>), a project of the Benton Foundation.

22. Levin and Arafeh (2002), 14–16.

Chapter 2

1. CEO Forum on Education and Technology (2000).

2. Leadership Conference (2002).

3. Holzer (1996), 3.

4. Twenty-first Century Workforce Commission (2000), 10, 23.

5. The University of Washington's Seattle/Port Elizabeth Digital Divide Project was conceived with the intention of creating awareness of the gap in technology between schools and communities in Seattle and Port Elizabeth. Students from the two cities were engaged in videotaped discussions about the role of technology in their lives and interacted with one another via videoconference. A video containing footage from the discussions and interactions was shown at a workshop entitled "Digital Divides, Digital Dividends" prior to the World Trade Organization's summit, held in Seattle in 2000. <http://www.washington.edu/eplt/devprojects/international/>.

6. Reder (1998), 1ff.

7. Educational Testing Service (2002), 2.

8. National Research Council (1999).

9. Wilhelm (1997), 143–144.

10. Bertelsmann Foundation (2002).

11. Goodman (2003), 24–31.

12. West (2002).

13. <http://www.puente.org/>.

14. <http://www.benefitscheckup.org/>.

15. U.S. Department of Commerce (2002b).

16. <http://www.scienceinafrica.co.za/2001/december/thinkquest.htm>.

17. <http://www.digitaldividend.org/pubs/pubs_01_akash_interview.htm>.

18. International Telecommunications Union (2002).

19. Gates (2000).

20. de Sola Pool (1983), 101.

21. International Commission for the Study of Communication Problems (1980), 192.

22. "No man is an island, entire of itself; every man is a piece of the continent, a part of the main." Meditation 17 from *Devotions upon Emergent Occasions* (1624).

23. <http://www.niti.org/html/cultural_preservation.html>.

24. Mandela (1996), 4.

25. U.S. Department of Commerce (1999), xiii.

26. <http://www.un.org/millenniumgoals/>.

27. Gittell, ed. (1998), 8.

28. <http://www.lincos.net>.

29. <http://www.american.edu/academic.depts/ksb/mogit/country.html>.

30. United Nations General Assembly (2001).

31. "No Child Left Behind Act of 2001," § 2402.

32. See <http://www.notschool.net/>.

33. National Center for Education Statistics (2002), 3; Bertot and McClure (2000), 3.

34. U.S. Department of Commerce, *A Nation Online* (2002a), 1.

35. *A Nation Online,* 10; Lenhart et al. (2003).

36. *A Nation Online,* 75.

37. Lenhart et al., xx.

38. *A Nation Online,*10.

39. *A Nation Online,* 36.

40. *A Nation Online,* 82.

41. *A Nation Online,* 17.

Chapter 3

1. McAfee, (2001), 36.

2. McAfee, 38.

3. IBM, for example, saves 70 percent of the cost of a service transaction when it is performed over the Net rather than in the paper or manual format. Altman (2001).

4. Armstrong and Casement (2000), 154–155.

5. Peter S. Goodman (2002).

6. Kurzweil (2000), 2–6.

7. Rifkin (1996), 71.

8. Consumer Federation of America et al. (2003).

9. For in-depth information on the government's growing surveillance apparatus, see the Electronic Privacy Information Center Web site at <http://www.epic.org/>.

10. Kau and Rubin (1979), 365.

11. For example, Marcuse (1964) writes, "The quantification of nature, which led to its explication in terms of mathematical structures, separated reality from all inherent ends and, consequently, separated the true from the good, science from ethics" (146).

12. Leavitt (1970), 4.

13. Atkinson (2002). For an alternative perspective on the virtues of increasing spending on smart public transportation projects to create a healthier community, see Sierra Club (2001).

14. Rifkin, 71.

15. For an example of downsizing in financial services, see Gosling (1999), 112, 116. In the blue-collar arena, at the end of 2002, longshoremen and shipping companies on the West Coast reached an agreement on the limited role of computer technology at ports; see Booth (2002).

16. The latest biennial review of media ownership regulations focused on the need to accumulate empirical research to justify the retention of rules limiting ownership that otherwise must be abolished. Under the influence of the law and economics approach, regulations serving the public interest must be empirically justified or be thrown out.

17. Staudenmaier (1995), 152–153.

18. Joseph Kahn (2003) writes, "In his 17 days of molding tool boxes, Wang Chengua learned to work like a metronome. He slipped strips of metal under a mechanical hammer with his right hand, then swept molded parts into a pile with his left. He did this once a second for a 10-hour shift, minus a half-hour lunch. Just before lunch on the 18th day, he lost the beat. The hammer, backed by 4,000 pounds of pressure, ripped through the middle and ring finger of his right hand, reducing them to pulp."

19. Rawls (1971), 86.

20. Rawls, 101.

21. Twenty-first Century Workforce Commission (2000), 23.

22. Sum, Fogg, and Mangum (2000), 23.

23. Barber (1994).

24. Organization for Economic Cooperation and Development (2002), 20.

25. Education and Library Networks Coalition (1999). Eighty-seven percent of respondents in a random sample survey of registered voters supported telecommunications discounts for needy schools and libraries.

26. AOL Time Warner Foundation (2003).

27. Lake Snell Perry & Associates (1999).

28. The White House (2000).

29. Eng (2001), 19.

30. Mitretek Systems (2003), executive summary.

31. Crandall and Jackson (2001), 47.

32. U.S. Government Working Group on Electronic Commerce (2000).

33. Dorr (2003), 5–6.

34. Association of Telehealth Service Providers (2001), 3.

35. Eng, 19.

36. Danzon and Furukawa (2001), 215.

37. Wang et al. (2003), 400.

38. Downs (1957).

39. Neuman (1991), 95–97.

40. Weiss (2003).

41. Litan and Rivlin (2001), 4.

42. Danzon and Furukawa, 215.

43. Whitten and Doolittle (2002), 18.

44. Gilson et al. (2002), 2.

45. Conte (2001), 23.

46. Schrank and Lomax (2002), 7–8.

47. Schrank and Lomax, 59.

48. Cohn (2003).

49. Schrank and Lomax, 61.

50. Krugman (2001).

51. Ferguson (2001), 55.

52. Crandall and Jackson, 36–37.

53. U.S. Environmental Protection Agency (2001), 1.

54. Texas Department of Telecommunications and Regulatory Affairs (1998), 7.

55. Auerbach (1999), 106.

56. Tennyson (1899), 333.

57. Kant's famous essay on perpetual peace anticipates Tennyson's remarks and embodies the Enlightenment faith in progress. Kant suggests that "the *spirit of commerce* sooner or later takes hold of every people, and it cannot exist side by side with war. And of all the powers (or means) at the disposal of the power of the state, *financial power* can probably be relied on most." Kant (1795), 114.

58. Horkheimer and Adorno (1947), 166.

59. Taylor (1997), 294.

60. Marx (1894), 441.

Chapter 4

1. Ivy Planning Group (2000), 2.
2. Navarrete and Kamasaki (1994).
3. Stanley and Steinhardt (2003), 11.
4. The White House (2002), sec. 7.
5. eEurope: <http://europa.eu.int/information_society/eeurope/2005/text_en.htm>; e-Envoy: <http://www.e-envoy.gov.uk/Home/Homepage/fs/en>.
6. Adopted and proclaimed by the Untied Nations General Assembly, resolution 217 A (III), December 10, 1948. Full text at <http://www.un.org/Overview/rights.html>.
7. For a state-by-state analysis, see the ACCESS Project's Web site at <http://www.accessednetwork.org/states/index.htm>.
8. <http://www.tifb.state.tx.us/>.
9. CEO Forum on Education and Technology (2001), 9.
10. "No Child Left Behind" Act of 2001, PL 107-110. <http://www.ed.gov/policy/elsec/leg/esea02/index.html>.
11. Education Week on the Web (2003), 58.
12. <http://www.cfequity.org/prday1.html>.
13. <http://election.com/uk/pressroom/pr2000/0312.htm>.
14. E-Government Act of 2002, H.R. 2458. <http://www.whitehouse.gov/news/releases/2002/12/20021217-5.html>.
15. "State Promotes Jobs Web Site Where Few People Use Computers," *Birmingham News,* November 29, 2002.
16. West (2002).

Chapter 5

1. Committee for Economic Development (2001).
2. The White House (2000).
3. U.S. Department of Education (2001).
4. For information on the E-rate program, visit <http://www.sl.universalservice.org/> and http://www.e-ratecentral.com/>.
5. Universal Service Administrative Company (2003).
6. See U.S. Department of Agriculture Web site at <http://www.usda.gov/rus/telecom/dlt/dlt.htm>.
7. Silvernail and Harris (2003), iii.
8. Baird (1999), 2.

9. National Center for Education Statistics (2002).

10. U.S. General Accounting Office (2001).

11. For other skeptical viewpoints on the seriousness of the digital divide agenda, see Compaine, ed. (2001).

12. Michalchik and Penuel (2003), 48ff.

13. Gilson et al. (2002), 1.

14. Frechtling et al. (2000), iii.

15. Industry Canada (2001).

16. eEurope: <http://europa.eu.int/information_society/eeurope/2005/text_en.htm>.

17. Since the 1996 Telecommunications Act eliminated the cap on nationwide radio station ownership, Clear Channel has grown from 40 stations to 1,240 stations, thirty times more than legislation previously allowed. Future of Music Coalition (2002), 24.

18. Murray (2003).

19. Lenhart et al. (2003).

20. Somerset-Ward and Anderson (2000), 48.

21. To track the debate on low-power radio, visit the Media Access Project Web site at <http://www.mediaaccess.org/>. In particular, the issue of whether low-power stations would cause unacceptable interference in the snug FM band underscores the conflict between media conglomerates seeking to monopolize the airwaves and public telecommunications producers who simply want to see media reflect the diverse aspirations of America's geography and communities of interest.

22. Similar to the low-power radio debate, the issue of spectrum management hinges on whether policymakers will continue to treat the electromagnetic spectrum as a proprietary right to be zoned and licensed or a shared good to be developed for the permanent use of the broadest array of public purposes. See New America Foundation's Spectrum Policy Program at <http://www.newamerica.net/>.

23. Universal Service Administrative Company, 31.

24. Snowe (2001).

25. Anderson and Becker (2001).

26. CEO Forum on Education and Technology (2001), 9.

27. Chow et al. (1998), ch. 5; U.S. Department of Commerce (1999), 47.

28. Fowells and Lazarus (2001).

29. Morino Institute (2001).

30. Carvin, ed. (2000).

31. Benton Foundation (1996), 25.

32. California State Senate. 2000. SB 1774.

33. Benton Foundation, 23.

Chapter 6

1. U.S. Department of Commerce (2002b).

2. Not-School.net is an online research project looking at ways of reengaging young people of school age into an environment in which they are able to develop new ways of learning. It is essentially a 24/7 virtual community, offering young people the opportunity to develop their self-esteem and expand self-directed learning, achieved through the support of tutors and mentors and the strategic use of information and communications technologies.

3. See Street-Level Youth Media, at <http://www.street-level.org/>,), a program educating Chicago's inner-city youths, including gang members and youths under court supervision, in media arts and emerging technologies for use in self-expression, communication, and social change. Street-Level programs build self-esteem and critical thinking skills for urban youths historically neglected by policymakers and mass media. Another project, called The Beat Within, is a weekly Web publication relaying the voices of young people from within juvenile hall. This outlet allows detained young people to express feelings of isolation and hope in connecting to a larger community within and without. <http://pacificnews.org/yo/beat/about.html>.

4. Comments made by Andrei I. Podolskij, professor of cognitive development at Moscow State University, at the Teens and Technology Roundtable II, Jacobs Foundation Communication Center, Öhningen, Germany, November, 7–8, 2002.

5. Pryor et al. (2002).

6. Gilliam and Bales (2001), 1. According to the authors, the three most frequently reported topics of youth news on local newscasts were crime victimization, accidents involving young people, and violent juvenile crime.

7. Organization for Economic Cooperation and Development (OECD) (2001), ch. 7.

8. Carvin, ed. (2000), 17.

9. Education Week on the Web (2003), 62.

10. Eurydice (2001), 26.

11. Levin and Arafeh (2002).

12. Computer-Training für benachteiligte Jugendliche. See <http://www.seniorenansnetz.de/> and <http://www.digitale-chancen.de/content/projects/indexdeep.cfm?key=278>.

13. See <http://www.youthlearn.org/> and <http://www.digitale-chancen.de/>.

14. Mergendoller and Moriarty (1999).

15. World Economic Forum (2002).

16. Anderson and Becker (2001), 5.

17. Eurydice, 10.

18. Adopted and proclaimed by the United Nations General Assembly, resolution 217 A (III), December 10, 1948. Full text at <http://www.un.org/Overview/rights.html>.

19. Gittell, ed. (1998).

20. OECD (2001), 57–58.

21. OECD (2001), 187–188.

22. OECD (2001), 118.

23. Livingston (2001), 33–40.

24. For a riveting account of the tension between traditional accountability measures and those made possible through small schools and smart use of technology, see Washor and Mojkowski (2003). As the authors write, "Most small schools feel a special responsibility to be accountable to the community, families, students, and themselves for each one of their children. Not only are they concerned about not leaving any child behind, but their practice of personalizing their schools with advisories, learning plans, internships, exhibitions, professional development, and portfolios aims to ensure that no child is left *unknown,* as a learner and as a person."

25. Gardner (2000).

26. Grob (2002).

27. Project TELL traced the effects of home computers with network access on the lives of disadvantaged students and their families over a seven-year period. Researchers followed a group of New York City public school girls and boys from low-income, minority families in segregated inner-city neighborhoods. One hundred and twenty-five middle school students scoring below proficiency on a standardized reading test were chosen, with an appropriate comparison group chosen from the same middle school. Results were not universally encouraging, particularly for severely at-risk students. For a subset of the treatment group, performance gains over four years were significant, and each person in the subgroup eventually graduated from high school and enrolled in local colleges. Kornblum (2001).

28. Grob (2002).

29. Center for Children and Technology (2000).

30. Curtis (2003), 8.

31. Blanchflower and Freeman, eds. (2000).

32. Breiter (2003b).

33. Blanchflower and Freeman, 403ff.

34. Wilhelm (2003).

35. Dickard (2002).

36. Murray (2003).

37. See <http://www.ed.gov/>.

38. Kubicek (1997), 387.

39. Federal Ministry of Education and Research (2000), 7.

40. For an overview of the E-rate program, see the Universal Service Administrative Company's Web site at <http://www.sl.universalservice.org/overview/>.

41. Federal Ministry of Economics and Technology and Federal Ministry of Education and Research (1999).

42. Federal Ministry of Economics and Technology and Federal Ministry of Education and Research, 9.

43. TNS EMNID (2001).

44. U.S. Department of Commerce (1999), xiii.

45. Lenhart et al. (2003), 3.

46. See <http://www.marktplatz-fuer-schulen.de/>.

47. Federal Ministry of Education and Research (2000), 8.

48. Federal Ministry of Education and Research (2002), 7.

49. National Center for Education Statistics (2002).

50. President's Committee of Advisors on Science and Technology (1997), sec. 3.1.

51. <http://www.webpunkte-bremen.de/>.

52. Breiter (2003a).

53. For more detail about the now defunct program, see <http://www.ed.gov/teachtech/>.

54. See note 25.

55. Finnish Ministry of Education (1999).

56. Finnish Ministry of Education (2001).

57. Nurmela, Parjo, and Ylitalo (2003), 14, fig. 2.5.

58. Eurydice, 10.

59. Finnish Ministry of Education (1999), sec. 1.1.

60. Nurmela, Parjo, and Ylitalo, 12, fig. 2.3; 24. According to the report, "The Finnish national economy relies heavily on the ICT sector, both in terms of value added and employment: on these measures there is no other OECD country where the ICT sector is more important."

61. Castells and Himanen (2002), 115.

62. Nurmela, Parjo, and Ylitalo, 35, fig. 3.16.

63. Nordic Council of Ministers (2002), sec. 2.2.

64. Nurmela, Parjo, and Ylitalo, sec. 3.3.

65. OECD (2001), , 58, 60, 308.

66. CEO Forum on Education and Technology (2001), 8. The report notes educational technology funding was less than 2 percent of total K–12 spending in 1999–00.

67. See http://www.21stcenturyskills.org/>.

68. President's Information Technology Advisory Committee (2001), 14.

69. For an exploration of the types of initiatives increased R&D dollars should be geared toward in the e-learning arena, see Kalil (2002).

70. CEO Forum on Education and Technology (2001), 9.

71. Wilhelm (2002), 294.

Chapter 7

1. Howe and Strauss (2000).

2. Rideout et al. (1999), 18.

3. Pastore (2002).

4. Kharif (2001).

5. <http://www.soundpartners.org/>.

6. For more information on the digital divide, visit the Benton Foundation's Digital Divide Network at <http://www.DigitalDivideNetwork.org/>. If you are interested in international digital divide issues, see <http://www.Digital Opportunity.org/>.

7. Wilhelm, Carmen, and Reynolds (2002), 3.

8. Attributed to the science fiction writer William Gibson.

9. Michael Wood (2002).

10. <http://blackplanet.com/>.

11. Brontë (1994), 12.

Conclusion

1. Freud (1930), 25.

2. Mill (1848), 5–6.

3. Rawls (1971), 102.

4. Diamond (1999), 255.

5. Mill (1859), 107.

6. Geller (1998), 227–228.

7. Schement and Forbes (1999).

Bibliography

Altman, Anne K. 2001. "Testimony before the U.S. Senate Government Affairs Committee on the E-Government Act of 2001." Washington, D.C. July 11. <http://govt-aff.senate.gov/071101_altman.htm>.

Anderson, Ronald E., and Henry Jay Becker. 2001. "School Investments in Instructional Technology." Irvine: Center for Research on Information Technology and Organizations, University of California, Irvine. <http://www.crito.uci.edu/tlc/findings/report_8/>.

AOL Time Warner Foundation. 2003. "Survey Finds Americans Concerned Young People Are Not Adequately Prepared for 21st Century Success." Press release, June 25. <http://media.aoltimewarner.com/media/fn_press_view.cfm?release_num =55253235>.

Armstrong, Alison, and Charles Casement. 2000. *The Child and the Machine: How Computers Put Our Children's Education at Risk.* Beltsville, Md.: Robins Lane Press.

Association of Telehealth Service Providers. 2001. *Report on U.S. Telemedicine Activity.* Portland, Ore.: ATSP.

Atkinson, Robert D. 2002. *Getting Unstuck: Three Big Ideas to Get Americans Moving Again.* Washington, D.C.: Progressive Policy Institute.

Auerbach, Jeffrey A. 1999. *The Great Exhibition of 1851: A Nation on Display.* New Haven: Yale University Press.

Baird, Zoë. 1999. "Improving Life in the Information Age." New York: Markle Foundation. <http://www.markle.org/news/presidents_letter.pdf>.

Barber, Benjamin R. 1994. *An Aristocracy of Everyone: The Politics of Education and the Future of America.* New York: Oxford University Press.

Benton Foundation. 1996. "Buildings, Books, and Bytes." Washington, D.C. <http://www.benton.org/publibrary/kellogg/buildings.html>.

Berkowitz, Bruce. 2003. *The New Face of War: How War Will Be Fought in the 21st Century.* New York: Free Press.

Bertelsmann Foundation and AOL Time Warner Foundation. 2002. "21st Century Literacy Summit White Paper." <http://www.21stcenturyliteracy.org/white/index.htm>.

Bertot, John Carlo, and Charles R. McClure. 2000. *Public Libraries and the Internet 2000.* Washington, D.C.: National Commission on Libraries and Information Science.

Blanchflower, David G., and Richard B. Freeman, eds. 2000. *Youth Employment and Joblessness in Advanced Countries.* Chicago: University of Chicago Press.

Booth, William. 2002. "W. Coast Shipping Contract Is Set: Deal on Technology Ends Bitter Dispute That Closed Ports." *Washington Post,* November 25, A01.

Breiter, Andrea. 2003a. "Public Internet Usage Points in Schools for the Local Community: Concept, Implementation, and Evaluation of a Project in Bremen, Germany." *Education and Information Technologies* 8 (2): 109–125.

———. 2003b. "Regional Learning Networks—Building Bridges between Schools, University, and Community." In *Informatics and the Digital Society: Social, Ethical, and Cognitive Issues,* ed. Tom van Weert and Robert K. Munro. Boston: Kluwer.

Brontë, Emily. 1994. "Remembrance." In *Emily Brontë: Selected Poems,* ed. Ian Hamilton. New York: St. Martin's Press.

California State Senate. 2000. SB 1774.

Carvin, Andy, ed. 2000. "The E-rate in America: A Tale of Four Cities." Washington, D.C.: Benton Foundation. <http://www.benton.org/publibrary/e-rate/e-rate.4cities.pdf>.

Castells, Manuel, and Pekka Himanen. 2002. *The Information Society and the Welfare State: The Finnish Model.* Oxford: Oxford University Press.

Center for Children and Technology. 2000. "The Transformation of Union City: 1989 to Present." New York. <http://www2.edc.org/CCT/admin/publications/report/uc_transform00.pdf>.

CEO Forum on Education and Technology. 2000. "School Technology and Readiness Report." Washington, D.C. <http://www.ceoforum.org/reports.html>.

———. 2001. "Education Technology Must Be Included in Comprehensive Education Legislation: A Policy Paper." Washington, D.C. <http://www.ceoforum.org/downloads/forum3.pdf>.

Chow, Clifton, Jan Ellis, June Mark, and Bart Wise. 1998. *Impact of CTCNet Affiliates: Findings from a National Survey of Users of Community Technology Centers.* Newton, Mass.: Community Technology Centers' Network.

Cohn, D'Vera. 2003. "Commuters Crossing Lines: Census Finds Majority Employed Far from Home." *Washington Post,* March 6, B01.

Committee for Economic Development. 2001. *The Digital Economy: Promoting Competition, Innovation, and Opportunity.* New York: Committee for Economic Development.

Compaine, Benjamin M., ed. 2001. *The Digital Divide: Facing a Crisis or Creating a Myth?* Cambridge, Mass.: MIT Press.

Consumer Federation of America et al. 2003. "Reply Comments in the Biennial Regulatory Review of the Commission's Broadcast Ownership Rules." Washington, D.C. February 3. <http://www.democraticmedia.org/resources/filings/>.

Conte, Chris. 2001. "Networking the Land: Rural America in the Information Age." Washington, D.C.: U.S. Department of Commerce. <http://www.ntia.doc.gov/>.

Crandall, Robert W., and Charles L. Jackson. 2001. "The $500 Billion Opportunity: The Potential Economic Benefit of Widespread Diffusion of Broadband Internet Access." Washington, D.C.: Criterion Economics.

Curtis, Diane. 2003. "Urban Renewal: The Union City Turnaround." *Edutopia* 1 (spring): 6–8.

Danzon, Patricia M., and Michael F. Furukawa. 2001. "Health Care: Competition and Productivity." In *The Economic Payoff from the Internet Revolution,* ed. Robert E. Litan and Alice M. Rivlin. Washington, D.C.: Brookings Institution Press.

de Sola Pool, Ithiel. 1983. *Technologies of Freedom.* Cambridge, Mass.: Harvard University Press.

Diamond, Jared. 1999. *Guns, Germs, and Steel: The Fates of Human Societies.* New York: Norton.

Dickard, Norris. 2002. "Federal Retrenchment on the Digital Divide: Potential National Impact." Washington, D.C.: Benton Foundation. <http://www.benton.org/publibrary/policybriefs/brief01.html>.

Donahue, Patricia L., Robert J. Finnegan, Anthony D. Lutkus, Nancy L. Allen, and Jay R. Campbell. 2001. "The Nation's Report Card: Fourth-Grade Reading 2000." Washington, D.C.: National Center for Education Statistics. <http://nces.ed.gov/pubs2001/quarterly/summer/q2-1.asp>.

Dorr, Thomas C. 2003. "Testimony before the Committee on Agriculture, U.S. House of Representatives." Serial No. 108-11. June 25. <http://agriculture.house.gov/hearings/10811.pdf>.

Downs, Anthony. 1957. *An Economic Theory of Democracy.* New York: Harper.

Education and Library Networks Coalition. 1999. *Connecting Kids and Communities to the Future.* Washington, D.C.: EdLiNC.

Education Week on the Web. 2003. "Technology Counts 2003: Pencils Down, Technology's Answer to Testing." <http://www.edweek.com/sreports/>.

Educational Testing Service. 2002. *Digital Transformation: A Framework for ICT Literacy.* Princeton, N.J.: ETS.

Elliott, Carl. 2003. *Better Than Well: American Medicine Meets the American Dream.* New York: Norton.

Eng, Thomas R. 2001. *The E-health Landscape: A Terrain Map of Emerging Information and Communication: Technologies in Health and Health Care.* Princeton, N.J: Robert Wood Johnson Foundation.

Eurydice. 2001. "Basic Indicators on the Incorporation of ICT into European Education Systems." 2000/01 Annual Report. Brussels. http://www.eurydice.org/Documents/TicBI/en/FrameSet.htm>.

Federal Ministry of Economics and Technology and Federal Ministry of Education and Research. 1999. "Innovation and Jobs in the Information Society of the 21st Century." Berlin. <http://www.bmbf.de/pub/inno21e.pdf>.

Federal Ministry of Education and Research. 2000. "Online-Offline: IT in Education." Berlin. <http://www.bmbf.de/pub/itkon_e.pdf>.

————. 2002. "IT-Ausstattung der allgemein bildenden und berufsbildenden Schulen in Deutschland." Berlin. <http://www.bmbf.de/pub/it-ausstattung_der _schulen_2002.pdf>.

Ferguson, Eric. 2001. "Three Faces of Eve: How Engineers, Economists, and Planners Variously View Congestion Control, Demand Management, and Mobility Enhancement Strategies." *Journal of Transportation and Statistics* 4 (1): 51–73.

Finnish Ministry of Education. 1999. "Education, Training and Research in the Information Society: A National Strategy for 2000–2004." Helsinki. <http:// www.minedu.fi/julkaisut/information/englishU/welcome.html>.

————. 2001. "A Wide Range of Culture and Quality Information Retrieval in the Library: The Salient Points and Proposals in the Finnish Library Policy Programme 2001–2004." Helsinki. <http://www.minedu.fi/minedu/>.

Fountain, Jane E. 2001. *Building the Virtual State.* Washington, D.C.: Brookings Institution Press.

Fowells, Linda, and Wendy Lazarus. 2001. *What Works in Closing the Technology Gap? Lessons from a Four-Year Demonstration in 11 Low Income California Communities.* Los Angeles: Community Partners.

Frechtling, Joy, Gary Silverstein, Kyle Snow, and Laurie Somers. 2002. "Technology Opportunity Programs: 1996 Projects." Rockville, Md.: Westat. <http://www.ntia .doc.gov/otiahome/top/research/EvaluationReport/1996_report_complete.pdf>.

Freud, Sigmund. 1930. *Civilization and Its Discontents,* trans. and ed. James Strachey. New York: Norton, 1961.

Future of Music Coalition. 2002. "Radio Deregulation: Has It Served Citizens and Musicians?" Washington, D.C. <http://www.futureofmusic.org/research/radiostudy .cfm>.

Gardner, Howard. 2000. *Intelligence Reframed: Multiple Intelligences for the 21st Century.* New York: Basic Books.

Gates, Bill. 2000. Keynote speech, Creating Digital Dividends Conference. Seattle, October 18. <http://www.gatesfoundation.org/MediaCenter/Speeches/BillgSpeeches/ BGSpeechDigitalDiv2-01018.htm>.

Geller, Henry. 1998. "Implementation of 'Pay' Models and the Existing Public Trustee Model in the Digital Broadcast Era." In *Digital Broadcasting and the Public Interest: Reports and Papers of the Aspen Institute Communications and Society Program.* Washington, D.C.: Aspen Institute.

Gilliam, Franklin D. Jr., and Susan Nall Bales. 2001. "Strategic Frame Analysis: Reframing America's Youth." *Social Policy Report* 15 (3): 1–16. <http://www .srcd.org/sprv15n3.pdf>.

Gilson, Preston, Ted Bannister, Michael Walker, and Brett Zollinger. 2002. "Evaluation Study of the Hays Medical Center Vital Signs In-Home Tele-Monitoring System Intervention for Chronic Obstructive Pulmonary Disease and Congestive Heart Failure Patients." Hays, Kan.: Docking Institute of Public Affairs, Fort Hays State University. <http://www.fhsu.edu/docking/img/Reportv11.pdf>.

Gittell, Marilyn J., ed. 1998. *School Equity: Creating Productive Schools in a Just Society.* New Haven: Yale University Press.

Goodman, Peter S. 2002. "China Serves as Dump Site for Computers: Unsafe Recycling Practice Grows Despite Import Ban." *Washington Post,* February 24, A01.

Goodman, Steven. 2003. *Teaching Youth Media: A Critical Guide to Literacy, Video Production, and Social Change.* New York: Teachers College Press.

Gosling, Paul. 1999. *Changing Money: How the Digital Age Is Transforming Financial Services.* London: Bowerdean.

Grob, Alexander. 2002. "Improving Learning and Professional Perspectives of Disadvantaged Adolescents by Peer Tutoring." Paper, Teens and Technology Roundtable II. Jacobs Foundation Communication Center. Öhningen, Germany. November 7–8. <http://www.digitale-chancen.de/transfer/assets/102.pdf>.

Grossman, Lawrence K., and Newton N. Minow. 2001. *A Digital Gift to the Nation: Fulfilling the Promise of the Digital and Internet Age.* New York: Century Foundation Press.

Holzer, Harry. 1996. *What Employers Want.* New York: Russell Sage.

Horkheimer, Max, and Theodor W. Adorno. 1947. *Dialectic of Enlightenment,* trans. John Cumming. New York: Continuum, 1994.

Howe, Neil, and William Strauss. 2000. *Millennials Rising: The Next American Generation.* New York: Knopf.

Industry Canada. 2001. "The New National Dream: Networking the Nation for Broadband Access." Ottawa. <http://broadband.gc.ca/pub/program/NBTF/index .html>.

International Commission for the Study of Communication Problems (MacBride Commission). 1980. *Many Voices, One World.* Paris: UNESCO. <http://article19 .net/docs.shtml>.

International Telecommunications Union. 2002. *Yearbook of Statistics.* Geneva: ITU.

Ivy Planning Group. 2000. *Whose Spectrum Is It Anyway? Historical Study of Market Entry Barriers, Discrimination and Changes in Broadcast and Wireless Licensing, 1950 to Present.* Washington, D.C.: Federal Communications Commission.

Kahn, Joseph. 2003. "China's Workers Risk Limbs in Export Drive." *New York Times,* April 7, A01.

Kalil, Thomas A. 2002. "An Information Commons for E-Learning: Designing a Digital Opportunity Investment Trust." Washington, D.C.: New America Foundation. <http://www.newamerica.net/Download_Docs/pdfs/Pub_File_848_1.pdf>.

Kant, Immanuel. 1795. *Perpetual Peace: A Philosophical Sketch,* ed. Hans Reiss. Cambridge: Cambridge University Press, 1970.

Kau, James B., and Paul H. Rubin. 1979. "Self-Interest, Ideology and Logrolling in Congressional Voting." *Journal of Law and Economics* 22 (2): 365–384.

Kharif, Olga. 2001. "Let the Games Begin—Online." *BusinessWeek Online,* December 13. <http://www.businessweek.com/technology/content/dec2001/tc20011213 _2329.htm>.

Kirsch, Irwin, John de Jong, Dominique Lafontaine, Joy McQueen, Juliette Mendelovits, and Christian Monseur. 2002. "Reading for Change: Performance and Engagement across Countries." Paris: Organization for Economic Cooperation and Development. <http://www.pisa.oecd.org/Docs/Download/reading_for _change.pdf>.

Kornblum, William. 2001. "The Digital Divide and the Severely At-Risk Student." Paper, Teens and Technology Roundtable I. Benton Foundation. Washington, D.C. October 4–5.

Krueger, Alan B. 1991. "How Computers Have Changed the Wage Structure: Evidence from Microdata, 1984–1989." Working Paper #291. Department of Economics, Princeton University. <http://www.irs.princeton.edu/pubs/pdfs/291.pdf>.

Krueger, Alan B., and Mikael Lindahl. 2001. "Education for Growth: Why and for Whom?" *Journal of Economic Literature* 39: 1101–1136.

Krugman, Paul. 2001. "Nation in a Jam." *New York Times,* May 13, op-ed.

Kubicek, Herbert. 1997. "Multimedia: Germany's Third Attempt to Move to an Information Society." In *National Information Infrastructure Initiatives: Vision and Policy Design,* ed. Brian Kahin and Ernest Wilson. Cambridge: MIT Press.

Kurtzweil, Ray. 2000. *The Age of Spiritual Machines: When Computers Exceed Human Intelligence.* New York: Penguin.

Lake Snell Perry & Associates. 1999. "Education and Digital Television: Seizing the Opportunity to Realize the Medium's Potential." Report on Findings from Focus Groups and a National Survey Conducted for the Benton Foundation. Washington, D.C. <http://www.benton.org/publibrary/television/edtv.html>.

Leadership Conference on Civil Rights Education Fund and the Benton Foundation. 2002. "Bringing a Nation Online: The Importance of Federal Leadership." Washington D.C.: Leslie Harris and Associates. <http://www.civilrights.org/publications/reports/nation_online/>.

Leavitt, Helen. 1970. *Superhighway—Superhoax.* New York: Ballantine Books.

Lenhart, Amanda, John Horrigan, Lee Rainie, Katherine Allen, Angie Boyce, Mary Madden, and Erin O'Grady. 2003. "The Ever-Shifting Internet Population: A New Look at Internet Access and the Digital Divide." Washington, D.C.: Pew Internet and American Life Project. <http://www.pewinternet.org/reports/pdfs/PIP _shifting_Net_pop_report.pdf>.

Levin, Douglas, and Sousan Arafeh. 2002. "The Digital Disconnect: The Widening Gap between Internet-Savvy Students and Their Schools." Washington, D.C.: Pew Internet and American Life Project. <http://www.pewinternet.org/reports/pdfs/PIP_schools_Internet_report.pdf>.

Litan, Robert E., and Alice M. Rivlin. 2001. *Beyond the Dot.coms: The Economic Promise of the Internet.* Washington, D.C.: Brookings Institution Press.

Litan, Robert E., and Alice M. Rivlin, eds. 2002. *The Economic Payoff from the Internet Revolution.* Washington, D.C.: Brookings Institution Press.

Livingston, Kay. 2001. "Disadvantaged Teenagers and Technology: Summary Results from a Transatlantic Research Inventory." In *Toward Digital Inclusion for*

Underserved Youth. Washington, D.C.: Benton Foundation. <http://www.benton .org/publibrary/ttr/TeenTechBooklet.pdf>.

Mandela, Nelson. 1996. Speech, TELECOM 95 Conference. *Trotter Review* 9 (2): 4–6.

Marcuse, Herbert. 1964. *One-Dimensional Man: Studies in the Ideology of Advanced Industrial Society.* Boston: Beacon Press, 1991.

Marx, Karl. 1894. *Capital.* Vol. 3 of *The Marx-Engels Reader,* ed. Robert C. Tucker. New York: Norton, 1978.

McAfee, Andrew. 2001. "Manufacturing: Lowering Boundaries, Improving Productivity." In *The Economic Payoff from the Internet* Revolution, ed. Robert E. Litan and Alice M. Rivlin. Washington, D.C.: Brookings Institution Press.

Mergendoller, John D., and Kevin Moriarty. 1999. "An Analysis of the Progress of the Idaho Educational Technology Initiative in Meeting Goals Established by the Idaho Council for Technology in Learning." Novato, Calif.: Buck Institute for Learning. <http://www.sde.state.id.us/Vault/DocVault/TechS/Mergendoller_Report _2000.pdf>.

Michalchik, Vera, and William Penuel. 2003. "Community Technology Centers Program: Case Study of Technology Access and Learning in Twelve Communities." Menlo Park, Calif.: SRI International. <http://www.ctl.sri.com/publications/ downloads/CTC%20Case%20Study%20Report.pdf>.

Mill, John Stuart. 1848. *Principles of Political Economy,* ed. Jonathan Riley. Oxford: Oxford University Press, 1994.

————. 1859. "On Liberty." In *Utilitarianism, On Liberty,* and *Representative Government,* ed. H. B. Acton. London: J. M. Dent, 1972.

Mitretek Systems. 2003. "Intelligent Transportation Systems Benefits and Costs: 2003 Update." Washington, D.C.: U.S. Department of Transportation. <http:// www.itsdocs.fhwa.dot.gov/jpodocs/repts_te/13772.html>.

Morino Institute. 2001. "From Access to Outcomes: Raising the Aspirations for Technology Initiatives in Low-income Communities." Reston, Va.: Morino Institute. <http://www.morino.org/divides/execsum_report.htm>.

Murray, Corey. 2003. "Budget Ax Falls on School Tech Programs." *eSchool News Online,* June 1. <http://www.eschoolnews.org/news/showStory.cfm?ArticeID= 4424> [registration required].

National Center for Education Statistics. 2002. "Internet Access in U.S. Public Schools and Classrooms: 1994–2001." Washington, D.C.: NCES. <http://nces .ed.gov/pubs2002/internet/>.

National Research Council. 1999. *Being Fluent with Information Technology.* Washington, D.C.: National Academy Press.

Navarrete, Lisa, and Charles Kamasaki. 1994. *Out of the Picture: Hispanics and the Media.* Washington, D.C.: National Council of La Raza.

Neuman, W. Russell. 1991. *The Future of the Mass Audience.* New York: Cambridge University Press.

"No Child Left Behind Act of 2001." 2001. Public Law 110, 107th Congress, January 8.

Nordic Council of Ministers. 2002. "Nordic Information Society Statistics 2002." Helsinki: Statistics Finland. <http://stat.fi/tk/yr/tietoyhteiskunta/nordic_iss_02.pdf>.

Nurmela, Juha, Lea Parjo, and Marko Ylitalo. 2003. *A Great Migration to the Information Society: Patterns of ICT Diffusion in Finland in 1996–2002.* Helsinki: Statistics Finland.

Organization for Economic Cooperation and Development. 2001. "Knowledge and Skills for Life." Paris: OECD. <http://www.pisa.oecd.org/knowledge/home/intro.htm>.

————. 2002. Financing Education—Investments and Returns. Paris: OECD.

Osborne, David, and Ted A. Gaebler. 1991. *Reinventing Government: How the Entrepreneurial Spirit Is Transforming the Public Sector.* New York: Perseus Books.

Pastore, Michael. 2002. "Demographics: Internet Key to Communication among Youth." *Cyberatlas,* January 2. <http://cyberatlas.internet.com/big_picture/demographics/article/0,,5901_961881,00.html>.

President's Committee of Advisors on Science and Technology. 1997. "Report to the President on the Use of Technology to Strengthen K–12 Education in the United States." Washington, D.C. <http://www.ostp.gov/PCAST/k-12ed.html#3.h>.

President's Information Technology Advisory Committee. 2001. "Using Information Technology to Transform the Way We Learn." Arlington, Va.: National Coordination Office for Information Technology Research and Development. <http://www.hpcc.gov/pubs/pitac/pitac-tl-9feb01.pdf>.

Pryor, Tisha, Katie McMillan Culp, Matt Lavine, and Jessica Hochman. 2002. "Evaluation of the Intel Computer Clubhouse Network: Year 2 Report." New York: Center for Children and Technology. <http://www2.edc.org/cct/admin/publications/report/Intel_CCN02.pdf>.

Ravitz, Jason L., Henry Jay Becker, and YanTien Wong. 2000. "Constructivist-Compatible Beliefs and Practices among U.S. Teachers." Irvine, Calif.: Center for Research on Information Technology and Organizations. <http://www.crito.uci.edu/tlc/findings/report4/report4.pdf>.

Rawls, John. 1971. *A Theory of Justice.* Cambridge, Mass.: Harvard University Press.

Reder, Stephen. 1998. "The State of Literacy in America." Washington, D.C.: National Institute for Literacy. <http://www.nifl.gov/reders/reder.htm>.

Rideout, Victoria, Ulla Foehr, Donald F. Roberts, and Mollyann Brodie. 1999. *Kids & Media @ the New Millennium.* Menlo Park, Calif.: Kaiser Family Foundation.

Rifkin, Jeremy. 1996. *The End of Work: The Decline of the Global Labor Force and the Dawn of the Post-Market Era.* New York: J. P. Tarcher.

Schement, Jorge Reina, and Scott C. Forbes. 1999. "Expanding the Menu: An Informed Choice Model of Universal Service for an Integrated Digital Environment."

Paper, 27th Annual Telecommunications Policy Research Conference. Arlington, Va., September 26.

Schrank, David, and Tim Lomax. 2002. "The 2002 Urban Mobility Study." College Station: Texas Transportation Institute, Texas A&M University. <http:// tti.tamu.edu/product/catalog/reports/mobility_report_2002.pdf>.

Sierra Club. 2001. "Clearing the Air with Transit Spending." The Sierra Club Sprawl Report. <http://www.sierraclub.org/sprawl/report01/>.

Silvernail, David L., and Walter J. Harris. 2003. "The Maine Learning Technology Initiative: Teacher, Student and School Perspectives, Mid-Year Evaluation Report." Gorham, Me.: Maine Education Policy Research Institute, University of Maine. <http://www.usm.maine.edu/cepare/pdf/ts/mlti.pdf>.

Snowe, Olympia. 2001. "Bridging the Digital Divide." Weekly Senate Update. Washington, D.C. March 30. <http://www.politicsol.com/guest-commentaries/ 2001-04-02.html>.

Somerset-Ward, Richard, with Rachel Anderson. 2000. "Connecting Communities." Washington, D.C.: Benton Foundation. <http://www.benton.org/publibrary/ publicmedia/pubmedia.pdf>.

Stanley, Jay, and Barry Steinhardt. 2003. *Bigger Monster, Weaker Chain: The Growth of an American Surveillance Society.* New York: American Civil Liberties Union.

Staudenmaier, John. 1995. "Henry Ford's Relationship to 'Fordism': Ambiguity as a Modality of Technological Resistance." In *Resistance to New Technology: Nuclear Power, Information Technology and Biotechnology,* ed. Martin Bauer. Cambridge: Cambridge University Press.

Sum, Andrew, Neeta Fogg, and Garth Mangum. 2000. "Confronting the Youth Demographic Challenge: Labor Market Prospects for Out-of-School Young Adults." In *The 21st Century Challenge: Moving the Youth Agenda Forward,* ed. Marion Pines. Baltimore: Sar Levitan Center for Social Policy Studies, Johns Hopkins University.

Taylor, Mark C. 1997. *Hiding.* Chicago: University of Chicago Press.

"Telecommunications Act of 1996." 1996. Public Law 104, 104th Congress, 110 Stat. 56 (1996), February 8.

Tennyson, Alfred Lord. 1899. *The Poetic and Dramatic Works of Alfred Lord Tennyson.* Boston: Houghton Mifflin.

Texas Department of Telecommunications and Regulatory Affairs. 1998. "Telework Pilot Project Final Results. Austin." <http://www.e-austin.org/telework-report .pdf>.

TNS EMNID. 2001. "Der Verweigereratlas—Basiserhebung." Bielefeld, Germany. <http://www.digitale-chancen.de/transfer/downloads/MD8.pdf>.

Twenty-first Century Workforce Commission. 2000. *A Nation of Opportunity: Building America's 21st Century Workforce.* Washington, D.C.: U.S. Department of Labor.

United Nations General Assembly. 2001. 56th Session. Resolution 56/116.

Universal Service Administrative Company. 2003. Annual Report 2002. Washington, D.C.

U.S. Department of Commerce. 1999. "Falling through the Net." Washington, D.C. <http://www.ntia.doc.gov/ntiahome/digitaldivide/>.

———. 2002a. "A Nation Online: How Americans Are Expanding Their Use of the Internet." Washington, D.C. <http://www.ntia.doc.gov/ntiahome/dn/>.

———. 2002b. "2020 Visions: Transforming Education and Training through Advanced Technologies." Washington, D.C. <http://www.technology.gov/reports/ TechPolicy/2020Visions.pdf>.

U.S. Department of Education. 2001. "Education Budget History Table." Washington, D.C. <http://www.ed.gov/about/overview/budget/news.html#history>.

U.S. Environmental Protection Agency. 2001. "Telecommuting/Telework Programs: Implementing Commuter Benefits under the Commuter Choice Leadership Initiative." Washington, D.C. <http://www.commuterchoice.gov/pdf/telecommute .pdf>.

U.S. General Accounting Office. 2001. "Telecommunications: Characteristics and Choices of Internet Users." Washington, D.C. <http://www.gao.gov/new.items/ d01345.pdf>.

U.S. Government Working Group on Electronic Commerce. 2000. Leadership for the New Millennium: Delivering on Digital Progress and Prosperity. Washington, D.C.: U.S. Department of Commerce.

Wang, Samuel J., B. Middleton, L. A. Prosser, C. G. Bardon, C. D. Spurr, P. J. Carchidi, A. F. Kittler, R. C. Goldszer, D. G. Fairchild, A. J. Sussman, G. J. Kuperman, and D. W. Bates. 2003. "A Cost-Benefit Analysis of Electronic Medical Records in Primary Care." American Journal of Medicine 114 (5): 397–403.

Washor, Elliot, and Charles Mojkowski. 2003. "Accountability in Small Schools: One Learner at a Time." <http://www.ecs.org/html/Document.asp?chouseid=4684>.

Weiss, Rick. 2003. "A Fight for Free Access to Medical Research." Washington Post, August 5, A01.

West, Darrell M. 2002. "State and Federal E-Government in the United States, 2002." Providence, R.I.: Center for Public Policy, Brown University. <http:// www.insidepolitics.org/Egovt02us.html>.

The White House. 2000. "The Clinton-Gore Agenda for Creating Digital Opportunity," February 2. <http://clinton4.nara.gov/WH/New/digitaldivide/digital2.html>

———. 2002. "The National Security Strategy of the United States of America." [Bush administration] <http://www.whitehouse.gov/nsc/nss.html>.

Whitten, Pamela, and Gary Doolittle. 2002. "Telehospice: A Bistate Proposal to Improve End-of-Life Care." Washington, D.C.: U.S. Department of Commerce. <http://ntiaotiant2.ntia.doc.gov/top/docs/eval/pdf/206099016e.pdf>.

Wilhelm, Anthony G. 1997. "Buying into the Computer Age: A Look at the Hispanic Family." In Proceedings of the Families, Technology and Education Confer-

ence, ed. Anne S. Robertson. Champaign, Ill.: ERIC Clearinghouse on Elementary and Early Childhood Education.

———. 2000. *Democracy in the Digital Age: Challenges to Political Life in Cyber-space.* New York, Routledge.

———. 2002. "Wire-less Youth: Rejuvenating the Net." *National Civic Review* 91 (3): 293–302.

———. 2003. "Leveraging Sunken Investments in Communications Infrastructure: A Policy Perspective from the USA." *The Information Society* 19 (4): 279–286.

Wilhelm, Anthony G., Delia Carmen, and Megan Reynolds. 2002. *Connecting Kids to Technology: Challenges and Opportunities.* Baltimore: Annie E. Casey Foundation.

Wood, Michael. 2002. "Teens Spent $172 Billion in 2001." Teenage Research Unlimited, 707 Skokie Blvd., Northbrook, IL 60062.

World Economic Forum. 2002. *Global Information Technology Report, 2002–2003: Readiness for the Networked World.* New York: Oxford University Press.

Index